Michael Law
Agility Matters

Published by: Business Agility Institute

Cover & Text Design: Michael Law
Graphics: Natalya English

ISBN: 978-1-957600-25-3 (print)
ISBN: 978-1-957600-26-0 (digital)

Print & Distribution: Kindle Direct Publishing

Agility Matters

A novel about adapting an organisation to
respond to customer needs, flexibly.

Michael Law

Contents

Preface

Why did I write this book

Over the last twenty years, I have seen many failed agile, digital, cloud and lean transformations. Many well-meaning executives have created a business case, designed the implementation strategy and then failed to deliver the net benefits promised. Not only this, but I see executives push media stories about how successful their transformations have been. Yet, when I analysed the transformation, I saw employees who were ready to leave and customers who didn't notice any changes.

I completed my thesis on customer value and business transformation for my executive MBA with Massey University in 2020. During the COVID pandemic, I continued researching, looking for a dynamic roadmap for success, the cheat sheet or a paint-by-numbers towards more engaged employees and more responsive customers. I found none.

I found that regardless of the term used to describe it, organisations are trying to keep pace with their customers' changes and are having difficulty determining what constitutes success. Additionally, there were common reasons for their failures.

Over the last decade, I have been involved with several transformations; the stories of what worked and when are in this book, and the pain points are covered by the fictional story of New Zealand Financial Services (NZFS).

This book has been written to give you hope; although there is no silver bullet, there is an iterative process filled with start-stops, similar conversations and a clear way forward.

Who is this book for

This book is designed for leaders. That does not mean someone with an executive title; a leader is someone who has followers. To obtain followers, you will have a clear vision and drive intrinsic motivation, which results in people working without the carrot or the stick.

This book does lean quite heavily toward technology; however, I urge you not to think of this book as a technology book. It is for leaders who see the future, who understand the customer is changing faster than their organisation, and those who can empathise with how this will impact the employees around them.

If you want a clearer understanding of how to measure your organisation's current state, create a vision for the future and a roadmap towards responding to the customer and employees' needs flexibly. If you want your people and organisation to have agility. Then this book is for you.

Where does it fit

Medium to large companies that have been through multiple transformations, are currently going through one or plan to transform. This book helps pave the way. Although value can be obtained for small businesses, there would be better books.

Medium to large companies have a high level of structure, process and complex factors that prohibit them from just stopping and changing direction. This is a business transformation book for organisations that should never go through a business transformation programme.

What problem does it solve

During my research, I found four critical problems during a transformation that meant they were set up to fail from the start. This book looks to solve the following issues so that you are set up to start adapting your organisation to respond to customer needs flexibly.

1) Not understanding your current state

If you go into the bush without a compass, you shouldn't be surprised that you spend the night cold, wet, and with a rescue helicopter the next day (true story), if you do not know where your organisation is, objectively, right now. Then you shouldn't move at all. Stay still and reassess.

Over the years, I found myself not enjoying transformations. The first question I ask "What metrics were we measuring before we began" was met with confusion and answers that are not metrics; "command and control", "lack of productivity", or "anywhere is better than here". This lack of current state gives no basis to measure empirically the changes you have made.

2) Lack of agreement on the metrics to hold the transformation accountable

Imagine patting yourself on the back after you finished a month-long diet and yet you didn't decide what success looked like? Were you successful because you didn't eat pizza for a month? If that WAS indeed your criteria, then congratulations. However, for most transformations, there is confusion on what metrics are being aimed for.

This book gives you some guidance around agility metrics. As your score improves on the leading indicators, you can then look to the customer or internal stakeholder metrics to validate that the lagging indicators match up and be confident this translates into better business outcomes through competitive advantages in your industry.

3) No clear vision for the future

The future is unclear, and yes, we are laying seeds; however, any team, business unit or organisational transformation needs a clear vision for what the end looks like, even if it is one that you never quite reach.

Agility is a little less clear than a goal to swim from one island to another, however, a guiding star, a vision of where we are heading, is a must-have. A vision should be so clear that everyone will shift automatically if something changes to achieve the same outcome. The critical difference between how the SAS was founded vs the territory army, was the idea that a plan is just one way to achieve the outcome, the plan changes, but the outcome doesn't.

4) Roadmaps that are static

It's almost funny if it wasn't scary. I have seen numerous agile transformations with roadmaps that were static. Just to be clear, agile is about accepting change, and yet some agile transformations cannot accept changes.

Any transformation involving people with any element of choice must have a dynamic roadmap. A focus on objectives, outcomes and outputs, prioritised beautifully with accurate capacity management, is a must-have. However, how does your plan change when people change their minds?

How can you use this book

This book is a novel, a story about Julie, who joins New Zealand Financial Services (NZFS). Although fictional in its portrayal, every conversation, pain point, solution and leader style in this book are taken from real people and actual events.

It follows the first three months of joining any organisation; the changes Julie makes may take you longer, and many buy-ins occur when there is pain, and the pain for Julie and NZFS is sped up for dramatic effect.

Each main section has academic research to lay the groundwork for learning. It will explain why things happen or how things can change, followed by Julie being able to implement elements of the research into NZFS due to the sudden pain they are experiencing. The research is academic, and the case studies and the results are real.

The book is divided into measuring the current state of an organisation split into four distinct values; Strategic Agility, Cognitive Diversity, Customer Experience and Employee Empowerment. You can do your own current state analysis for free here:

www.AgilityMatters.nz.

Continuing on from the agility values, which allow the organisation to measure where they are now and make plans to improve, key performance indicators are created based on customer and internal stakeholder metrics. Allowing an organisation to measure accurately the impact of changes they have made.

The last section of the book helps the reader identify how

to combine all competing priorities into one prioritised list; in the NZFS case, the triple o model (Objective, Outcome and Outputs), the same model can be used for an Agility Transformation. It introduces an adaptive strategy model called the seven circumstances of strategy and helps the reader create a dynamic roadmap for success.

This book does not focus on organisational transformation. It focuses on helping leaders make iterations to their current state of agility, current measurements for both leading and lagging indicators, a way to deliver CAPEX and OPEX value to their customers in a prioritised and data-driven way, and provides an adaptive strategy to keep changing with the needs of your customers in a flexible way.

For more information, see our website:
www.AgilityMatters.nz

Or find us on YouTube:
https://www.youtube.com/@agility_matters

Acknowledgements

This book would not have been completed without other people in my life. Firstly to my wife Lucy and children, Benjamin, Alexander and Daisy. I do not have much spare time, and you put up with me sitting alone to write, research and analyse.

To my mother, who raised my sister and me by herself while constantly trying to maintain some sort of career. Without the knowledge passed down to me from Lorraine, I would not question everyone and everything.

The Surge Whanau, every single one of you, past and present, have been asked to read a chapter, review or just help me with ideas. Thank you: www.SurgeConsulting.co.nz

Cohort one from my first Business Agility Foundations course. I created a course for ICAGILE on business agility, and the questions asked over those three days led me to promise you this book. Without that promise, I would have stopped.

Agility Matters

Day 1

Discovery

"Congratulations, you got the job!"

Julie knew she would always remember this moment. She gripped the phone tight against her head and steeled herself to respond. Behind her, her kids were arguing over what programme to watch in their two-bedroom apartment in Auckland, New Zealand.

Julie was a thirty-four-year-old mother of two who'd recently finished her Executive MBA with Massey University. Four weeks ago, out of the blue, she'd been headhunted for a General Manager of Technology role within a large financial company called New Zealand Financial Services - or NZFS, as they liked to be called.

It was a dream job. And for Julie, it wasn't just about the money, the career prospects, or the passion she had for the industry. It was also the fact she wouldn't have to work from home anymore! Her current workplace had closed its offices during the Covid pandemic and never reopened them, expecting all technology staff to work from home if they weren't client-facing. Julie missed the 'brain switch' she often felt when she walked into a workplace, mentally and physically separating her personal life from her work life. And she missed the banter of the office, the brainstorming, the friends she made during difficult times...

"Are you there, Julie?" the hiring manager sounded worried.

Julie almost gasped out her response: "Yes, absolutely! When can I start?"

"I expect you'll need to give four weeks' notice," the hiring manager said.

"Yes. But I might be able to negotiate something else."

The hiring manager laughed. "I like your enthusiasm. We'd love to have you as soon as you can, Julie!"

They talked a little about the logistics of her start date and ended the call with promises to keep in touch about any updates. Julie set down the phone and then allowed herself a quiet "Yes!" fist-pump - quiet so that the kids wouldn't hear. She'd break the exciting news to them later.

Kids, Mummy's just landed her dream job...

This was, Julie decided, her big chance - a real opportunity to use everything she'd learned in her working life. She wasn't short of experience. After leaving school at sixteen, Julie worked in a range of different jobs across many fields and industries. She'd been everything from a supermarket supervisor to a Ruby-on-Rails developer.

However, something had always been missing. It wasn't the pay - she had always been happy with that. But every time she left a job, she'd never felt as if she'd achieved what she wanted to. Whether it was in the boardroom or a factory back office, she felt her ideas were ignored. Although she was competent - and well-regarded wherever she went - she had never experienced real joy at work.

Staring outside the window of her apartment, she knew with confidence she'd never felt before - that it would be different at NZFS. This time she could create a team like whānau (family), and they could drive towards better outcomes for their customers and themselves.

New Zealand onboarding processes are not normally quick, but Julie found herself walking through NZFS's security gates within two weeks of the phone call. At the reception, she was levelled some hard questions, to which she had to give some awkward answers - no, I don't have a laptop, no I don't have a pass with a photo on it - but eventually, she was given a Visitor's pass and sent up to Level 28 to meet Gregory, the Chief Information Officer (CIO), whom she'd briefly met three weeks ago in her interview.

Although Julie was excited, she was also very nervous. Not only was this a new job, but NZFS had recently been in the news for privacy breaches and system failures.

Auckland, Feb 8 (NZ Herald) - New Zealand Financial Services (NZFS) Head office said on Tuesday a hacker attack overnight had disrupted its services but assured its customers that their personal data had not been compromised as a result of the incident, which is under investigation.

New Zealand Financial Services said in a statement its system faced technical problems on Monday evening, with thousands of customers reporting they were unable to access their accounts or pay their bills on their phones or computers.

Eager to learn as much about the company before she joined as she could, Julie had read every article she could find, but all were big on sensational claims and scant on the actual details. It made Julie wonder what sort of problems she was walking into.

First Day at NZFS

Gregory had a solid handshake and wore a banker's suit. He was exactly as Julie remembered him - charismatic and confident. His office was well-appointed but not overly flashy.

"Welcome aboard, Julie," he said, gesturing to her to sit. "I'm excited to have you working for me. Let me give you a quick summary... and the bad news. My team is eight strong, with three hundred employees reporting directly or indirectly to them. Your predecessor hired three direct reports, but they have since left, which means you currently have three teams of people reporting directly to you. I hope you are up for the challenge?"

Immediately alarm bells triggered inside Julie's head. Why have people left? Why are there eight leaders for three hundred people? Also, why am I working FOR Greg, not WITH Greg...?

She pushed these worrying thoughts aside. "Absolutely! Who

doesn't like a good challenge?" she replied, determined to keep her good humour and, more importantly, to make a good impression.

"Excellent news." Greg laughed. "Your desk is on Level 27 with the other members of technology leadership. The executive team are here on Level 28, and employees are spread throughout this building and our building on the north shore - it's only thirty minutes away by Uber. I've left the welcome pack on your desk as you haven't got a laptop. It'll explain the vision for our company and the strategy we are currently implementing. Have fun, and again, welcome aboard... Oh, I need to take this call. Excuse me."

His phone was ringing; he picked it up. He turned away from her to take it. Julie took this as a dismissal. So this would be the whole of her welcome: a short and not-very-sweet introduction to NZFS. In fact, it was much, much shorter than Julie would have liked.

Greg was already telling her a lot about how the company worked.

Travelling down the stairs to Level 27, Julie decided to "walk the floor". Greg was clearly not going to introduce her to people right now, and she wanted to get the flavour of her colleagues in a more informal fashion. She passed from desk to desk, offering a hello, a smile, and a quick explanation of her presence: I'm Julie, the new Technology Manager.

Everyone she met seemed to be a senior leader in a different part of the organisation. This meant that on a floor of forty people, there were roughly thirty senior leaders. All were formally dressed - snappy suits and ties for the men and severe blazers for the women.

Current Strategy & Vision

Finding her desk wasn't difficult: it was the one with flowers and a large welcome aboard pack. She opened the pack and was pleasantly surprised by the contents. The vision and strategy were amazing. Polished. Succinct. The vision talked about the customer as the key stakeholder and how employees were empowered to be the best they could be. The strategy included plenty of smiling faces with cheerful quotes from employees.

"Three years old, that one!"

Julie looked up to see a man wearing jeans and a T-Shirt - instantly out of place among his sharp-suited colleagues.. His accent was strongly south-islander. He grinned at her.

"Hey, I'm Mark; I am the Customer Experience General Manager... or General Manager Customer Experience... or something like that."

It must have been the perplexed look on Julie's face that made Mark continue: "You've seen our strategy, I see. Every three years, the executive team brings in a big four consultancy to redo it. I'm assuming that due to the problems we have had this year, the latest edition has been delayed."

"If this strategy is pre-Covid, what is the current strategy?" Julie asked.

Mark laughed. "Look, a vision statement is something you could create with an online generator of keywords."

Julie smiled. "You mean something like...

Our mission at NZFS is delivering great customer service with sincerity, pride and innovation!"

"Yep. Goals are created every three years with consultants to align with what the board wants to see, which is a greater return on equity than the previous three years. We do have a yearly strategy. Last year we had one hundred and thirty-one strategic initiatives."

"How many did you complete?" Julie asked.

"Nine, but we did have forty-five in progress. We would have eventually completed them, but then Covid happened, and the direction changed. Those forty-five have been cancelled. We'll be redoing the strategy in three months, so you've got time to try and wiggle in something strategic sounding to get a budget."

That sounded ominous. After Mark left, Julie returned to reading her welcome pack. Reading between the lines of the strategic documents, it seemed Mark was telling the truth. Each year NZFS prepares business cases for strategic initiatives. The highest return on equity was prioritised.

The rules for business cases were simple:
- The initiative must be completed in the financial year,
- Business cases must be presented the month before they began, and
- There could be no outside spending.

All this meant was that Julie would have three months to fight for a budget for a team she hadn't even met.

Meeting the team
Julie's first-day welcome included a morning tea in the Level 8 kitchen. She took the stairs down - in part to increase her step count, but mainly so she could see her new workplace in action. The floors she saw were filled with workflow boards, cubicle-style desks, organisational strategy posters, and technology framework

diagrams she recognised.

Fifteen people were waiting to meet her on Level 8. They began introducing themselves before she'd had a chance to grab a sausage roll. Out of habit - Julie had been introduced to many, many people in her career - she began to separate them into groups in her head to help her remember who they were.

The first to welcome her were the project managers. There were four of them, all men in their forties, who seemed genuinely happy to see her. Unfortunately, they had similar names - Steve G, Steve M, Shaun, and Stan. Or was it Stan G and Steve C? This may be a problem, Julie thought to herself.

Next up were six business analysts of various genders and ethnicities - much easier for Julie to remember. One business analyst, Susan, began to apologise almost as soon as she'd said hello.

"So nice to meet you, Julie, but I can't stay! I'm on a facilitation course right now and just nipped out for your meet-and-greet."

"Don't worry about it," said Julie. "Facilitation is a fabulous skill to have. How did you decide which course to take?"

Susan's body language changed slightly; she looked briefly uncomfortable. Then she explained, "I didn't choose it. It came out of my performance review. We get feedback based on our previous quarter's outputs. Then our manager books the courses for us to upskill on what he thinks we're lacking."

"Oh, okay. That sounds... helpful." In truth, it sounded strange to Julie, but she bit her tongue. She didn't want to undermine anyone's authority on her first day. "I'll see you later, Susan."

The last group she met were standing together, hoarding the sausage rolls and pies. Mainly men, this group wore rock band T-shirts, were mostly bearded, and froze as Julie approached them.

Ah, Julie thought. The developers.

She knew many senior managers had trouble relating to technical members of their teams. But she had done a stint as a Ruby-on-Rails developer and knew first-hand what it was like to work in a technical role. She began the conversation with a quick hello, then quickly shifted to 'shop talk', asking questions about the technologies and methodologies the team were using to deliver. Even though her coding knowledge was out of date by now, Julie could see the team were warming to her simply because of her interest in and appreciation of what they did.

"We're glad to get a new GM," said Simon, who'd introduced himself as the technical lead of the integration team. "Especially as you're a technical GM and not a…."

"Not a hands-off leader?" Julie jumped in.

"You said it, not me," said Simon.

They all smiled, which made Julie feel more at ease.

Julie was able to gather a lot of information from the developers - who called themselves technical leads at NZFS. There were actually five teams, not three, and each team had a specialisation. Simon drew a quick picture for her on a nearby whiteboard.

The teams were:
- Integration Team
- Business Support Team
- Front-end Development
- Back-end Development
- Testing and Quality and Assurance

Each team had a technical lead. Business analysts floated between teams. Project managers drove most of the strategic initiative work.

Simon explained: "We are one big team of thirty. Work comes in via the project managers. Each project manager represents one area of the business. Business analysts make sense of what the business needs. Then we make it happen."

The technology department seemed to operate purely for its internal stakeholders - who everyone seemed to call the customer. Julie also noticed that Simon didn't include the project managers and business analysts as part of "the team". Maybe because they reported to another manager?

Before everyone went back to their desks, Julie had one more question for Simon.

"What about the end customers?" she asked. "Who are they?"

Simon shrugged. "The end customer? All of New Zealand, I guess?"

"Oh..."

Julie must have looked so crestfallen at his answer that Simon quickly added, "There's a strategy and design team on Level 18. They probably have detailed customer stuff." He grinned sheepishly. "We don't know much about that kind of thing; we're just developers."

"Thanks so much for your help, Simon," said Julie. "I'll check them out later."

Finding The Customer

Level 18, home of strategy and design, was very different from the other floors Julie had seen. Instead of desks, there were 'collaboration zones' filled with whiteboards and photos of people Julie guessed were those elusive end customers. Julie found what she was looking for behind a flip-board on wheels.. A collection of customer personas!

A customer persona is a fictional person whose identity and needs can be used to represent a group of people an organisation focuses their attention on. NZFS had six types of customers, each with their own pain points, desires and experiences:

"Are you looking for someone?"

A frazzled-looking woman had appeared behind Julie and was now glaring at her.

"I'm Julie, the new General Manager of Technology," Julie explained. "Sorry for poking about, but I was told this was the place to get information on our customers."

Instantly the frazzled woman switched from a glare to a broad smile. Again, Julie was taken aback by how fast people warmed to those who took an interest in their work. She expected that Level 18 didn't get many visitors besides people who wanted to steal post-its.

"Nice to meet you, Julie. I'm Jude. I work in process design. We've created some core customer profiles here and over there- "

She pointed to a rather dusty process diagram on the far wall

"- are their journeys. They show how our products match the problems the customers have."

Julie went over to study the diagram. "This is fantastic work, Jude," she said. "You and your team should be very happy. I can see the entire journey of the customer. How often are customers brought in to update these journeys?"

And also, she thought, why isn't this customer journey map in every General Manager's welcome pack?

Jude deflated a little. "They don't, not really. My boss, Mark, has tried to get other technology leaders to buy into designing products around their customers. But most of the work the technology folk do is reactive. You know, something breaks because there's an upgrade to one of our connecting systems, so we have to fix it. Or one of the leaders or a board member reads something in a magazine and decides we should have it, too. When they make a change, we update these processes and flows."

Julie guessed Mark-the-boss was the t-shirt and jeans wearing General Manager, Customer Experience. She smiled.

"So what about the customers?" she asked. "Do they have a voice?"

"We get feedback from a survey that goes out to all customers after we launch a new product or feature."

Julie could tell Jude knew this wasn't ideal, but Jude also seemed resigned to the fact that this was how things worked at NZFS. Julie was starting to realise the size of the issues she would have to overcome if she wanted to achieve her goals.

Technology Leadership Team

Julie's final meeting on her first day was a leadership meeting. She was looking forward to finding out what was in motion. The meeting was being officially held in a boardroom, but half the leadership team had tuned in via video call.

Greg, the CIO, dialling in from what seemed to be his office just one floor away, opened the meeting. "Hello, everyone. I'd like to take this chance to welcome Julie to our team."

There were some awkward claps and smiles... but no return introduction for Julie to learn the names of her new colleagues.

"Let's crack on then, shall we," said Greg. "Who's up first to talk about their space?"

Julie had nothing to contribute to this session, which gave her a chance to observe what was being said and how it was being said. Each leader, when prompted by Greg, spoke for around fifteen minutes about their work. The only exception was Mark. He went second and succinctly stated his update in under a minute - what he'd done that week, what he was working on, and the challenges he was facing. The others waffled on about this problem and that problem, and the more she heard, the more Julie worried.

Her first concern was the amount of work that seemed to be going on. Each of the leaders was accountable for their initiatives, but there were so many in progress! As this was the last quarter of the financial year, most initiatives should have been completed already. So far, only nine had been - just as Mark had told her earlier. All the leaders were claiming their projects were on track to complete on time... but Julie doubted it.

These projects were likely watermelon projects: a project which is reported to senior managers as "green" or "good" until someone digs a little deeper and discovers that underneath the surface, the project is "red" - i.e. in deep trouble.

Julie also noticed that all the leaders were using the word 'value' differently. When Mark talked about value, he was talking about customer satisfaction. Other leaders talked about value as a measure of financial savings, or lowering risk, or return on equity... and for about a third of the initiatives, Julie couldn't work out what the project's 'value' was at all.

She could see that this had led to other problems. All the projects had a backlog of work to do - that is, a list of uncompleted work that should be prioritised so that the work that is of greatest value is prioritised and completed first. The lack of a common measure of value meant it was impossible to know what work should be given priority.

As a result, it seemed as if everything was urgent... which technically meant that nothing was urgent.

It got worse. A lot of the projects in play seemed to be made up of must-have features - with no benefit realisation plan to obtain value earlier. This meant that NZFS would see no change for its customers or processes unless the entire project was completed. So, if the project were shut down early, NZFS would get no results!

No wonder Mark was upset about stopping the initiatives last year! Julie thought. It would have meant nothing was available to the customers. Just waste.

But the most confusing thing to Julie was how these leaders delivered outcomes. Listening in, Julie began to mentally sketch out the flow of the work the teams did in her head.

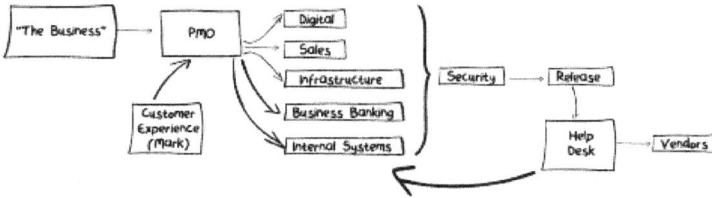

Although the strategic initiatives made Julie's head hurt, she did get to hear about how they delivered the outcomes. Digital had scrum teams created for each initiative, the leaders would create the solution with the architect team, who would then give the solution to the teams to break down into smaller tasks, which is then part of their backlog. A backlog is a list of uncompleted work that is prioritised for the greatest value first. Lastly, it seemed that each initiative went through multiple leaders as they were dependent on each other. So much for scrum?

Julie couldn't hold it in any longer. "Everyone is having similar problems with the delivery model," she burst out when the last leader had finished their update. "What is the process for improving it?"

There was a sudden silence. Everyone looked up at Greg on the conferencing screen - it seemed he was the only person able to answer the question.

"Great question, Julie," he said. "The Chief Financial Officer has a Project Manager's Office - the PMO. They have process improvement specialists. We make recommendations to them, but they have a large backlog to get through. We're hoping that we can re-look at the delivery process in quarter one."

He was smiling at her, but Julie knew better than to rock the boat any further.

"Thanks, Greg," she said. "That's great to know."

Home was calling. Julie took a longer route to walk home, giving herself a chance to think about everything she'd experienced. She was still determined to achieve her goals at NZFS... she just needed to understand what goals would be best to start with.

After the kids were in bed, Julie curled up with a fresh glass of Australian Shiraz and grabbed her textbooks from her MBA. Her first step, she decided, was to understand the current state of the organisation - its people, its processes and its technology.

Week 3
Current State

Observe with empathy

For the next three weeks at her new job, Julie didn't try to change anything. She simply observed.

This was not because she felt she somehow knew better than everyone else at NZFS, or because she didn't believe she could make an impact. She simply wanted to understand what was going on. As a leader, Julie knew that if she wanted to make changes, she would have to come from a place of empathy rather than a place of authority. She had to understand why NZFS was the way it was, and why people had let this state of affairs continue, even though many seemed to know it wasn't working.

Every few days, she would receive notifications of "Priority 1" or "Priority 2" issues that required her approval, decision, or support. People would urgently request her to "decide on our vendor contract by the end of the day" or say "If we don't get the okay to deliver this now, eight other projects will have to stop." It was difficult for her to determine the level of urgency for these problems and which ones should be addressed first. Furthermore, the constant shifting of priorities made her feel like she was on a rollercoaster.

"We're not helping our team with all this context-switching," Julie explained to a perplexed project manager, who had presented her with three Priority 2 issues in a single day. "If we keep changing priorities and making our teams work on multiple pieces of work at the same time, then they'll have to keep changing their focus and end up delivering sub-optimal results," she added.

The project manager's name was Steve G. He was around 45, round, with grey hair (likely caused by the constant shifting of priorities) and was shorter than Julie. "I have six high-priority items and only two teams! How can I deliver if no one is working on them?" he exclaimed.

"If everything is urgent, then nothing is urgent. Choose the highest priority with the shortest deadline or flip a coin, but just focus on one thing per team," Julie replied.

Steve was clearly not pleased, but he shrugged and returned to his desk.

~

Steve was correct, everything was indeed urgent. Even after three weeks of observing how the teams operated, Julie couldn't find a way to measure the value of their activities and determine which "priority" was more important than the others. A failure to identify worthwhile work was hurting NZFS more than they realised. In the modern business world, Julie knew customer expectations were changing rapidly, and NZFS had no ability to adapt to them.

Julie spent what felt like a few hours trying to manage a Priority 2 issue in her integration space. When she finally had a chance to look at the clock, she saw it was 3 pm. She realised she hadn't managed to grab lunch all week.

Just then, Mark appeared on her instant messenger tool. "Breakfast?" This was Mark's way of being funny, but Julie didn't find it funny anymore. "I'm going to have a packet of chips and a coke at my desk," Julie typed back. "Feel free to join me." Two minutes later, Mark was sitting beside Julie's desk with a pristine tofu salad and a smoothie.

"So how's it going? I heard you've had a few... um, incidents recently," Mark said.

"It's ridiculous," Julie admitted. "There hasn't been a day since I joined that I could catch my breath. The teams that do our business-as-usual operations are constantly slammed with requests, both project-related and unique incidents. The integration team seems to try and do work for any part of the business that asks, which means they don't spend any time maintaining the systems. My development and testing teams aren't really teams at all, they just work on random things the project managers or other leaders give them. Everyone's working hard, but nothing is getting done."

She took a long sip of her coke. "Apart from resolving some technology incidents, which all seem to be a P1 or a P2, I don't think we delivered anything valuable in the three weeks I've been here. And I doubt we're going to deliver anything valuable in the next three weeks, either," she said.

"Structure," Mark said smugly.

"What do you mean, structure?" Julie snapped back.

"Our organisation isn't designed right," Mark said simply. "You've got too many masters. Sure, Greg is the CIO, but technology is just seen as a glorified help desk, and he's done nothing to stop that. There are projects in every part of the organisation, not just technology. You're fighting against an entire company full of people who need your people, so you're going to keep bouncing around and watching your systems slowly fall apart," he explained.

"I know this! And you know this. But what can we do to fix this?" Julie asked.

Understanding The Past

Mark stopped mid-bite, put his fork down and looked genuinely distraught. "There was a time I thought I could fix this," he said. "I was hired based on my knowledge and performance at a previous company. So I started off running workshops, got a bit of buy-in, but then it all fizzled out. I was told there were too many priorities to focus on, to waste time changing how we operated. Now I spend my time trying to mitigate issues and stop people from leaving. And it kills me because I'm actually good at getting organisations to structure themselves to perform better."

"What do you mean?" Julie asked.

"Okay, maybe I'm teaching you to suck eggs here, but let me explain," Mark said. "To be productive, organisational structure, strategy, and processes should be focused around the customers themselves. That allows organisations to move with changing demands and create new products fast in response to the customer, without having to rely on other teams and get bogged down in politics."

"Makes sense to me," Julie said.

"Now let's talk about NZFS," Mark continued. "As a financial organisation, they haven't seen much competition, regulations, or disruption. It's made them complacent. The way the organisation is structured once gave them a competitive edge, but now it isn't suited to the way modern customers think. Customers want quick responses to their problems, and they don't care about our internal priorities or value chains or whatever else we've come up with. Our staff are going to start quitting in droves."

Julie remembered reading about these things in her MBA. Organisational design that once gave a competitive advantage had now created barriers to growth. If NZFS didn't start prepping for the future, it would be in trouble. New, disruptive organisations would arrive, like Uber, who'd taken market share, or Amazon, which dominated multiple value chains, or Apple, which kept customers purchasing incremental variations of its products.

Successful companies understand their value chain. A value chain is an end-to-end value a customer obtains while solving a problem they have. In other words, companies that understand what the problem is they solve, have a better chance of developing products or services that solve that problem and ensuring each step provides value to the customer.

Value chains help identify the flow of value but are misunderstood. They are not customer journey maps, which are customer-centric and provide experience-focused deliverables. They are not for internal stakeholders as they are customer-focused and they are not processes. They are a view of the system of value! Something we don't have at NZFS, Julie thought.

"Mark, my concern isn't people leaving," Julie said. "My concern is that we're going to be completely destroyed by better, smarter local competitors and bigger, more powerful global players! They'll take our market share and our employees."

"I see I have a new champion to fight the good fight," Mark said. "But I've tried to convince people, and it hasn't worked. Look, let me find my old pitch document."

He jumped onto her computer and began fiddling about in the file system. Finally, he opened a document - a document that seemed to have been buried within multiple different folders - and ushered her in to read.

Julie started reading aloud: "Disruption has increased since the 1960s with technology, culture, and globalism evolving rapidly. The current environment is volatile, uncertain, complex, and ambiguous (VUCA)[12]. Companies that once were dominating the field have been disrupted. Companies like Kodak, Blockbusters, and TomTom have been pushed aside by Apple, Netflix, and Google.

The ability to understand customer needs instead of company needs allows companies like Netflix to drive innovation faster than their competitors. Continuously disrupting themselves, Google's rapid evolution, leveraging data to interpret aggregate customer needs, allows them to change their strategy to match. Apple brings in real customers to test their products before release, to ensure they solve a problem.

Although there are many ways to approach this, one powerful method is to understand the customer's value chain. A value chain is an end-to-end value that a customer obtains while solving a problem they have. By understanding this, a company can develop products or services that solve that problem and ensure each step provides value to the customer.

NZFS needs to start preparing for the future by focusing on their customer's value chain and be ready to adapt to the changing demands of the market. If they don't, they risk being left behind by their competitors. "

Julie looked up from the document, deep in thought. "I understand now. We need to start thinking about our customers and their needs, not just our internal priorities. I'll start working on this right away."

"That's the spirit," Mark said, smiling. "I knew you were the right person for the job."

Julie knew that it wouldn't be easy, but she was determined to help NZFS adapt to the changing market and stay competitive. She knew that by understanding the customer's value chain and making it the focus of the organisation, they could create a sustainable future for the company.

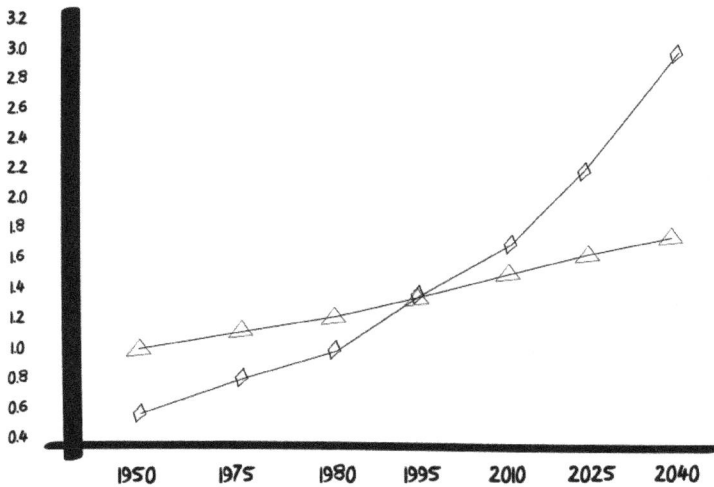

"Right now, this company and the world outside it are moving too fast for a deliberate strategy, As you can see here, the rate of change due to technology is growing at a faster rate then the ability for a human to adapt over time." Julie said. "We need to focus on a vision for NZFS that allows us to respond when we need to, in the ways we need to. We need to be agile, but we also need to be strategic. We've got to explain why this is important, what problem it solves, and then prove it using data. Are you in, Mark?"

"Sounds like fun," Mark replied with a smile.

"Great," Julie said, glancing at her emails. "I'll see you tomorrow for a proper breakfast, and we can talk more about Strategic Agility. But for now, it looks like Steve needs me to deal with another priority issue."

Julie knew that it was important to be able to adapt quickly to changing circumstances and to implement strategies that will help the company achieve its vision. By focusing on a vision that allows for strategic agility, the company can respond to changing market conditions and stay competitive. She was excited to work with Mark to develop a plan that would help NZFS thrive in the fast-paced, ever-changing business world.

Culture Enables Technology

Bright, and early the next morning, Julie met Mark in the company's cafe. She'd come armed with post-its, print-outs, a whiteboard on wheels, and a lot of information she'd read over the previous night from her MBA papers. Mark had come armed with coffee.

"Great, let's dive in," Mark said, taking a sip of his coffee.

Julie began her presentation. She explained to Mark that creating a culture that supports and encourages the use of technology is essential for staying competitive in today's market. She emphasised that technology is constantly evolving and changing, but if the culture within the organisation is not conducive to embracing new technology and innovation, it will be difficult for the company to keep up.

"The key is to focus on the customer's value chain," Julie said. "We need to understand the problems our customers are facing and how we can use technology to solve those problems and provide value to them. This is where we need to start, and it will help us to be strategic and agile in our approach."

Mark nodded, taking notes as Julie spoke. He was impressed with her passion and understanding of the subject. He realised that perhaps he had been too focused on trying to change the structure of the organisation and not enough on the culture.

"I think you're right," Mark said. "We need to focus on the culture and how it can enable technology. It's a fresh perspective and I'm excited to see where this takes us."

As they finished their discussion, other employees started to gather around, curious about what was being discussed. Julie and Mark realised that their conversation was not only helping them but also creating interest and engagement among the employees.

"Let's keep this conversation going," Julie said. "And let's involve more people in this change, we can't do it alone."

Mark agreed, and they decided to schedule another meeting with the rest of the team to discuss their plans and gather input and ideas. They knew it would be a challenging journey but they were determined to make it happen.

"I'm always open to learning new things."

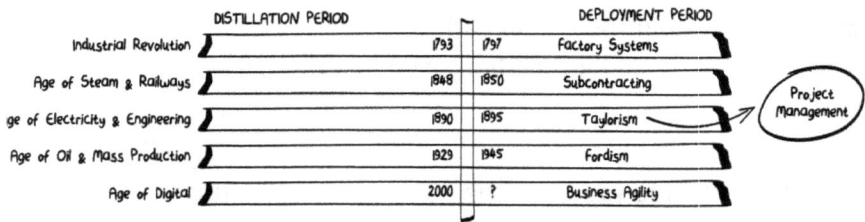

	DISTILLATION PERIOD		DEPLOYMENT PERIOD	
Industrial Revolution	1793	1797	Factory Systems	
Age of Steam & Railways	1848	1850	Subcontracting	Project Management
ge of Electricity & Engineering	1890	1895	Taylorism	
Age of Oil & Mass Production	1929	1945	Fordism	
Age of Digital	2000	?	Business Agility	

Adapted from Sooner Safer Happier | Jonathan Smart

"Exactly," Julie said. "Henry Ford's quote about faster horses, highlights the importance of understanding the customer's culture and what they truly want, not just what they say they want. That's why we need to focus on understanding the customer's value chain and their problems, and use that knowledge to drive innovation and development.

That's why I've drawn this chart," she said, pointing to the whiteboard. "The red line represents the product adoption curve, or the percentage of people who want the product. The blue line represents the product development curve, or how much the product has changed and developed over time. As you can see, the two lines are closely related. The more closely aligned our product development is with the customer's culture and needs, the more successful our product adoption will be."

Mark nodded, understanding the concept. "So, you're saying that by understanding the customer's culture and what they truly want, we can drive innovation and development, and ultimately increase product adoption?"

"Exactly," Julie said. "It's all about understanding the customer and creating a culture within our organisation that supports and encourages innovation and development. That's how we'll stay competitive in today's market."

Mark was impressed with Julie's understanding of the subject and her ability to explain it in a clear and concise manner. He realised that in order to be successful, they needed to create a culture that supported and encouraged innovation and development, and that it was essential to understand the customer's culture and what they truly wanted. He was excited to work with Julie and the rest of the team to create a culture that would enable technology and ultimately drive success for the company.

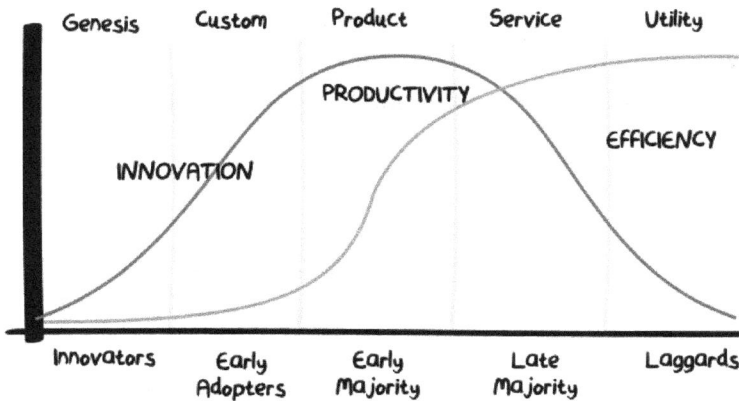

"Every product goes through an evolution from early innovation through to commoditization. As competition enters a Market, it drives the prices down, standardised features appear and eventually the innovation becomes common practice and a utility, which in turn boosts more innovation. This aligns nicely with the product adoption curve, where innovators want to test new things and early adopters enjoy being first. Then comes the early majority which makes it not so cool anymore, and eventually when a late majority hits, the early adopters have already found something new to focus on."

"And then at the end, even the most anti-car person seems to admit they want a car," Mark said. "You know, Henry Ford did not invent the automobile, nor the assembly line. Ford leveraged the work of Federick Taylor to take 300 odd variations of custom automobiles and turn it into a product that the early majority could get behind.

If however, the culture was not ready, it would have failed, just like the electric car did in 1890," said Julie.

"Tesla is doing well now," Mark pointed out.

"Let's talk about organisational culture," Julie said, not willing to be swayed off track by Mark's obvious interest in cars. "There are five different types of organisations I want to discuss."

"According to whom?"

"Mark, if you want to, you can have all my books and you can read them yourself. I am mostly leveraging the work of Frederic Laloux from the book 'Reinventing Organisations' for the types of culture and Dave Snowden from his book 'Cynefin', pronounced ki-nef-fin; it's Welsh. Dave has done some great work splitting the types of work into five separate domains. Clear, Complicated, Complex, Chaotic and Confused. We can ignore confusion, the other four suit our business rather well, there are things that we do that we understand fully, they are clear, we have created best practices for them and we know these because we sense when something is easy to do, categorise it almost automatically and then respond with said best practice, make sense?"

Mark nodded. "Complicated items are not so Clear" Julie smiled until she realised that yet again her humour didn't work on Mark "complicated environments are when we understand the route to complete the outcome, we use good practices like in accounting to sense the outcome we need to achieve, analyse the correct response and then respond. Complexity is multifaceted, we don't always know how we will do something, so we probe the problem first to understand better, which allows us to get a sense of what to do and then respond. Interestingly enough, Dave Snowdan also mentions that oscillating between complicated and complex has the best outcome. You start with complex, commoditise the complexity into good practices and then innovate to create more complexity. Which I like. Overall Complex is emergent, i.e it is not planned, it emerges from innovation or events or changes in the customer/technology that we can not control. "

"Makes sense, so what is chaotic?" Mark writing on the whiteboard as Julie talks

"Chaotic environments require completely novel processes, you must act first. Like Covid in 2020, we needed to close the borders, go into lockdown and ACT quickly with novel processes, then sense and then respond with an appropriate deliverable."

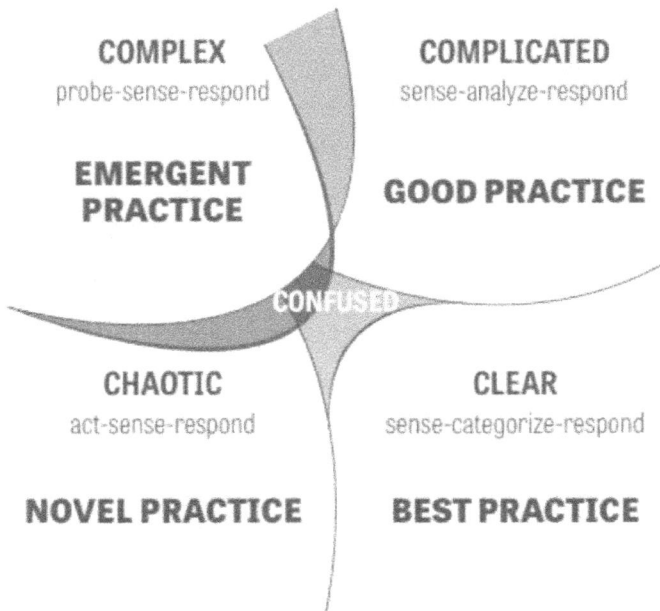

COMPLEX
probe-sense-respond

COMPLICATED
sense-analyze-respond

**EMERGENT
PRACTICE**

GOOD PRACTICE

CONFUSED

CHAOTIC
act-sense-respond

CLEAR
sense-categorize-respond

NOVEL PRACTICE

BEST PRACTICE

Dave Snowden | thecynefin.co

"Anyway I am combining three years of reading and I am giving you cliff notes" Julie eyed him. When he didn't respond, she continued: "Originally there was magenta organisational culture. These organisations didn't have any strategy or vision. It's just one long fight for budget and support."

"We have a strategy and vision by a big four company. Probably cost us a lot, so we aren't magenta. I suspect no organisation today is magenta but it gives us a bottom line."

"Then there's red culture. Back in the early industrial revolution, organisations were run by fear. If you didn't do what the boss wanted, you were sacked and that likely meant you starved, meaning a high level of compliance. It was a highly reactive and short-term focused culture which could only thrive in simple environments. We might see these organisations in the Mafia or ISIS. Or a family business that wonders why it can't grow!"

"We don't want NZFS to be red," said Mark helpfully. "What's the next colour?"

"Amber is the type of culture you'd see in most organisations these days. They have highly formal roles within a hierarchical structure and paternalistic leadership. They thrive in environments where efficiency is a competitive advantage. Think of the church, schools and government."

Mark nodded. "Is that the culture we have here at NZFS?"

"I suspect so. However, we need to prove it. We also need to understand the culture of our chosen customer to see if we match."

Mark stood up and walked over to the whiteboard, which now resembled an artist's canvas - Julie had been scribbling as she talked. "If Red works for managing simple tasks, and amber works for efficiency or complicated tasks, what about productivity or complex tasks?"

"Efficiency is all about the yield between inputs and outputs. For example, how many kilometres I can get out of a litre of petrol? Petrol in, kilometres out. Productivity is about value over time. An example of this would be how many parcels are delivered per day for customers. Yes, petrol efficiency is required, but if you had a very efficient car but you weren't delivering very many parcels, you would have an efficient process but an unproductive system. Productivity allows people to focus on the outcome and not the process. This is Orange's organisational culture."

"That sounds like my area," said Mark. "Finding out what the customer wants as an outcome. Do you know the key difference between Ford and Toyota? Henry Ford was quoted that a customer could have any colour they wanted, as long as it was black. Toyota would only paint based on the demand from the customer. Ford was more efficient but Toyota was more productive. Once the culture turned and the bulk of people wanted choice, only Toyota could properly serve them."

Mark clearly loved cars and was now drawing the lifecycle of cars on the whiteboard.

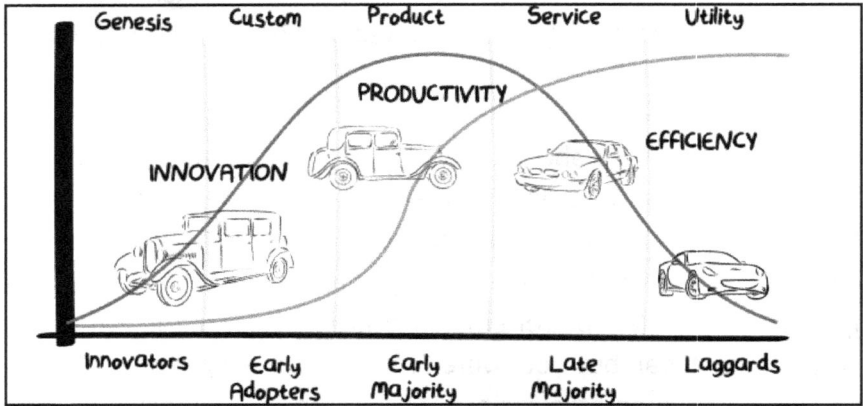

Genesis	Custom	Product	Service	Utility

PRODUCTIVITY

EFFICIENCY

INNOVATION

Innovators	Early Adopters	Early Majority	Late Majority	Laggards

Mark explained: "So, we had early bike companies making early innovative automotive. Ford realised that for cars to be mass Marketing they needed to be made cheaper and productionised. Then Toyota understood the culture and forfeited efficiency for productivity. And then remaining car manufacturers automated car manufacturing but added on innovation elements like Tesla, which started the cycle again. So the automobile followed the process from genesis to utility, and the companies who were successful at each part of the journey changed the features based on the culture of the customer at the time!"

Julie clapped. "Absolutely. Now you're starting to understand green organisations or agility culture."

During the 1990s we saw the speed and rate of change increase (Volatility), and increase in potential surprises (Uncertainty), the solutions are now multifaceted due to industries converging (Complex) and the difference between ideal vs actual is diverging (Ambiguity), these problems organisations face are coined as VUCA, as your presentation illustrates. Research has shown that the risks can also be mitigated by VUCA. Creating a Vision of the future, Understanding things will change, providing Clarity to customers and employees and Agility; the ability to adapt an organisation to respond to the customer's needs in a flexible way."

Mark suddenly looked dismayed. He slumped back into his chair and picked up his forgotten coffee. "This is interesting, sure," he said. "Thanks for teaching me about this. But I don't see how your research is going to help. NZ Financial Services are different. It's not a utility, like a car. How would we turn NZFS into the Tesla for financial services?"

Julie smiled. "Wherever you go on a trip there are three key pieces of information you need:
- Where you are now
- Where you are going
- How do you propose to get there?

"Our first step is to know exactly where we are before we look at where we are going. Then we can see if these changes are aligned with our customers, if green is the end goal from our point of view, we need to measure value and stop when we reach a plateau."

"From what I've learnt academically and in previous roles, I believe there are four key areas for us to focus on to allow us to adapt NZFS to respond to our customer's needs in a flexible way:

1. Strategic Agility - The ability for an organisation to pivot quickly to events that happen.
2. Cognitive Diversity - The ability for the right people with the right skills to deliver value.
3. Customer-Centricity - The ability to focus on the customer, for the customer and with the customer.
4. Employee Empowerment - The ability to decentralise decision making to maximise customer value.

I'm going to send you some information on strategic agility to your inbox. Take notes, there'll be a test tomorrow."

It was only when she began packing up her things that she realised her little talk had gathered quite an audience. A couple of people smiled and nodded at her as she left. She wasn't sure how long they'd been listening, but she took it as a good omen.

Week 4
Strategic Agility

Strategic Planning Isn't Dead

In 1994, Mintzberg declared the death of strategic planning. However, strategic planning has continued to evolve and is still in high demand. Strategic planning is used by management to increase performance[3].

A recent meta-analysis of strategic planning by George, Walker and Monster in 2019 had a more extensive data range of 31 studies over twenty years. Their findings found a moderate correlation to operational performance through strategic planning.

Effective performance of an organisation does not show that the organisation is delivering financial performance. George et al. show us there is a negative correlation to financial performance. While evaluating George et al., it can be seen that since the 1990s, organisations have moved from financial models of success to key performance indicators that are not financially focused. This could be due to 'performance effectiveness' allowing management to appear victorious in their strategy even though the organisation's outcomes, efficiency and financial correlations are a weak correlation with strategic planning. If management was to focus on effectiveness, then strategic planning is advantageous. George also found that there were greater outcomes with strategic alignment over planning, that is to have a single vision for the organisation.

When expanding correlation to innovation and flexibility, something organisations need in order to stay relevant in a changing world, Dibrell, Clay, Justin, Craig and Neubaum study in 2014 shows weak correlation between the firm's performance and formal strategic planning but also weak correlations between flexibility in strategic planning, innovation and performance. The key area of focus of the latest meta analysis shows us that flexibility is more correlated to successful outcomes than rigid planning.

Although Strategy planning may have a weak correlation with performance, the organisations that had consistent strategic alignment have benefited the most.

Strategic planning is made up of many qualities. It is found that flexibility of a company and how often that company adapts to the external information has a positive correlation on performance[4]. Each cycle is different for organisations and needs to be continuously revisited for maximum optimisation of resources.

Yousaf and Majid found that strategic performance was more significant when the organisation was aligned. For the ability to align, organisations required relationship skills, trust, cooperation and coordination as a team. Yousaf and Majid found that the network can not lead to a performance by itself, as the teams naturally create a vision where it lacks[5]. Thus we know that without sufficient vision from leadership, the tribal culture will fill the void in its place.

The ability for an organisation to have a single vision set by leadership, allows teams working together to align and deliver strategic performance.

Strategic performance is a closer measure than business performance, as it has measurements for the long term success of an organisation.

When evaluating qualities against strategic planning, there is sufficient evidence to show strong organisational networks, strategic alignment and flexibility are required for strategic performance over strategic planning and innovation.

Although there is no registered intellectual property to the term strategic agility, there is a common understanding that it is the ability to pivot quickly with the Market instead of using long term forecasts[6]. This definition would allow a set of qualities instead of processes to be used to measure strategic agility.

Weber discusses that strategic agility is essential in a complex world. Organisations that adapt quickly to complex problems use rapid learning processes, changing how they deliver based on external factors[7]. Agile organisations are flexible with their strategy, awaiting new information from external factors.

Morton, Stacey and Mohn discuss strategic agility from an IT leader's point of view. Essential qualities found that clear visions that empower teams to be flexible on how they are delivered are more successful.

Morton et al. focussed on 20 semi-structured interviews with IT leaders that had successfully implemented strategic agility. Interviewees reported not only flexibility and adaptation as crucial skills but also being the change leader and changing the culture to trial and error while maintaining strategic alignment with the CEO[8].

We can simplify all factors that lead to strategic performance in a complex environment as strategic agility. Creating a vision for constant change in a complex environment, leaders can create strong networks in their organisation, which leads to more significant innovation and strategic alignment.

Strategic agility enables strategic planning to be flexible and regularly revisited, a clear organisational vision is leveraged by all and the organisation adapts based on customer needs. (agile leadership).

~

As Mark finished reading what felt like a scientific journal, he could tell Julie had put some thought into this.

Everything is Urgent; Nothing is Urgent
The next morning Mark found Julie at her desk, where she was clearing out her emails - long streams of P1 and P2 emergencies.

"I think I get it," he said, before she could even get out a hello. "There are five types of organisational cultures, and if your organisation's culture matches the culture of your customer, you set yourself up to serve them better than anyone else can."

"That's about it," Julie said, nodding.

Mark continued, "So, it follows that if we want NZFS to respond to our customers' needs in a flexible way, we need to start working towards creating that culture. First step is to measure where we are now, so that we can objectively move in the right direction. We need to focus on understanding four key areas: Strategic Agility, Cognitive Diversity, Customer-Centricity and Employee Empowerment."

Julie gave him a little clap. "Correct, those were the four key areas I focused my MBA research on. All seemed to lead to greater business outcomes for organisations. Our job now is to figure out how to objectively measure each of those and h– oh, blast.." Her phone was ringing. "It's Steve," she told Mark, and picked up the phone.

"Hello?"
"Julie, it's Steve.""Steve, how can I help?"

"I have four projects, all urgent. Each business leader says they're a priority, and two are demanding that I stop everything else because they paid for us."

Julie had been noticing how managers at NZFS seemed to think that working with her scrum teams had the same dynamic as working with an external IT vendor.

"Also, we have a new problem," Steve went on. "One of the teams is not doing any of the projects as they are working on their own work. I need you on level 11 immediately to resolve this."

He hung up the phone before Julie had a chance to protest.

~

Steve hadn't specified where or which meeting room on level 11 he would meet her in. There was no need. When she stepped onto the floor, Julie immediately saw the epicentre of the drama: a 'modern workspace' grandstand area beside the kitchen. The grandstand's back wall was made of TVs all linked together, and was surrounded by fifty or so chairs. Currently there were over thirty people sitting in or standing around.

The grumbling began the moment she opened her mouth.

"Hello everyone," Julie said, approaching the group with a sense of apprehension.

Steve emerged from the throng. "We have a priority issue," he blurted out. "There are only two months left in the financial year and we seem to have five competing priorities for our people! As I said to you yesterday, I want to have the teams working on four of them, which are the approved projects. We won't finish them by the end of year but we will take a big chunk out of them, which will reduce the effort for next financial year, but now Simon is saying he needs the teams to work on technical debt!"

He turned to face the crowd. "Julie recommended working on one thing, the most important thing first, which I thought was a great idea. However, after talking to everyone, it seems that all these projects as important to each other and I think we would all rather be working on them all."

Playing the hero while throwing me under the bus, Julie thought, narrowing her eyes. We will talk about this later, Steve.

A tall and slim fellow in the group rose to his feet. He was wearing a banker's suit and accountant's glasses. His name, Julie recalled, was Patrick - the head of the enterprise project management office. He was originally from France and Julie quietly suspected he exaggerated his native accent for attention.

He was also Steve's manager.

"Nice of you to join us, Julie," Patrick said. "Let me recap: we have four projects, all approved by the executive leadership team, all a high priority. Yet you are recommending stopping three, and to add fuel to the fire, your team has prioritised business as usual activities over capital projects worth millions. Can you explain why? Maybe we missed something?"

Patrick's passive aggression was spot on. Julie looked past him and noticed all the stakeholders were there, from every project her teams were meant to be supporting. Even Henry the Chief Marketing Officer had made an appearance.

She took a deep breath. "If everything is urgent, nothing is urgent," she said in a calm voice. "You are all here because your projects are at risk. I understand your concern. Trust me, if I could ensure that all projects would be delivered by the end of year, I would. However, there is no way to deliver all your projects by the end of the year, and we all know there is a risk you will not get the budget to complete your project next year."

Now that got everyone's attention. They shifted in their chairs uncomfortably. Julie had hit their fears dead on.

Capacity Management

"The reason we have this issue," Julie said, "is because we work on everything at once. We constantly move back and forth between projects. We try to keep everyone happy by working on their projects, but working on a project won't mean you will receive any benefits sooner. It only means it is being worked on. Most likely, you will wait much longer than if my team could dedicate all their time to completing one project at a time."

Julie walked over to one of the giant TV screens and flicked it to whiteboard mode."Simon, how much time does it take to maintain our department? I mean, in terms of looking after our systems, keeping them updated so the lights stay on."

Simon clearly didn't like suddenly being involved, but thought about it for a moment. "About 50-60% of our time is maintaining our systems. It's why we need to stop working on projects for a week. We've been spending 90% of our time on projects for the last few months, and now have a heap of technical debt, urgent issues, and we've got a primary API that's not working for our customers."

That bit of news changed the vibe in the grandstand even more. A major API down? Even the most eager project owner knew how important it was for NZFS's customers to ensure they have the data they needed to make financial decisions. Why would you try to change your business with projects when your current services weren't working?

"Do you have enough people on that priority, Simon, or do you need to go?" Julie asked.

"It's fine. I think we need to sort this out now before the process gets worse."

Julie returned to her whiteboard. "So we have thirty people, eight weeks and five days a week, assuming no holidays... which means we have 1200 working days capacity within my team. To maintain our current services, we need to keep 720 of those days free to work on business as usual updates and fixes. I'm going to ring fence those hours, as maintaining the services of our current customers is far more important than working on projects. Henry, would you agree?" Henry was a young executive, only forty-two. He had blonde hair in a bun, wore a suit a size too small and often didn't wear socks. He always reminded Julie of someone on their way to the beach, not a member of a financial company. But Julie had always felt he was smarter than some of the other executives around the table. " Yes, I'd agree," said Henry. "What's more important than the reputation of the company? Our current customers must receive their products and services first, before we try to add more. Can you imagine what the news would say about us if more of our services broke?"

It had been a risky move to pull him into the debate. Julie hid her delight that he had agreed with her. She began drawing on the whiteboard.

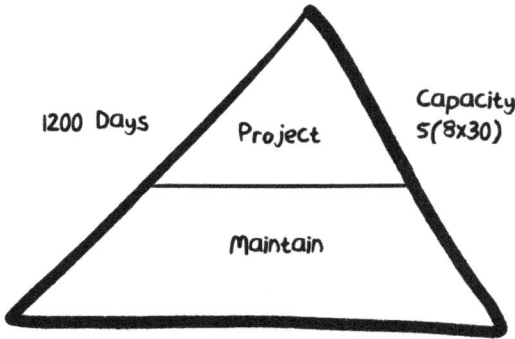

"So that's 720 days earmarked for maintenance," Julie confirmed to her audience. "There's one other thing I want to call out here. We currently do not do any continuous improvement activities - that is, improving the services we already have. Continuous improvement would have a higher return on investment. This is because we have already spent the capital allocation on the features we are maintaining, and by definition, continuous improvement is about reducing our maintenance costs. So that's something we need to focus on next year since 60% of our time is spent on maintenance."

She frowned at the board. "This leaves us with 480 days capacity between now and the end of the year. Steve, do you have a list of the must-haves for each project, and how long they're projected to take to complete?"

Steve reluctantly walked over to the whiteboard screen and opened his spreadsheets up.

Project A - 940 days
Project B - 865 days
Project C - 147 days
Project D - 350 days

"These are the projects waiting for your team to finalise. All these projects have been worked on by numerous other teams across the organisation, we just need you to finish and release them."

Julie stood back and stayed quiet, letting her audience soak in the numbers. It was evident there was only capacity to deliver one, or maybe two projects, by the end of the year. Splitting the capacity across all four projects would mean they would deliver none of them.

"You've told me all these projects are equally important. Does this mean they all have a similar return on equity percentages?"

Julie was being sneaky here, as she already knew there was no benefit realisation plan.

There was a deadly silence. Then each stakeholder and project team tried to explain what was in their business case, trying to make the case that their project was most important. Each time they tried, Julie would gently ask them for numbers. Each time the stakeholders mumbled something along the lines of: "There's no way to quantify the benefits."

"Right," said Julie, after all the project stakeholders had stuttered to a standstill. "Let me explain our situation. We have four projects that have been deemed to be our highest priority, yet none have quantifiable financial or non-financial data for us to validate. I propose we create a rough idea of value for each project, relative to other projects."

The stakeholders agreed, some looking a little shamefaced. They took turns to explaining benefits of their projects as they saw them. Even Patrick began getting involved. This time Julie didn't question them - she just wanted them to listen to each other.

At the end, Julie was able to place each project on a relative line.

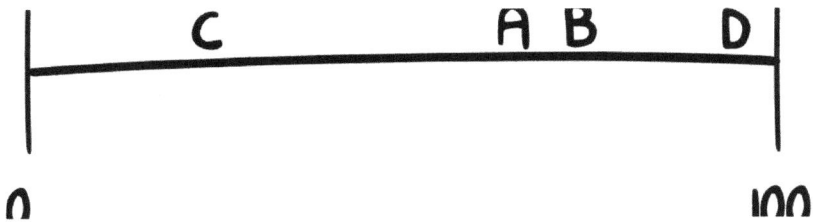

To everyone's surprise, the largest project, Project A, had fewer benefits than Project B or D, both of which cost substantially less. Julie was aware there were sunk cost issues but that was a problem for another day. Today she just wanted a clear direction.

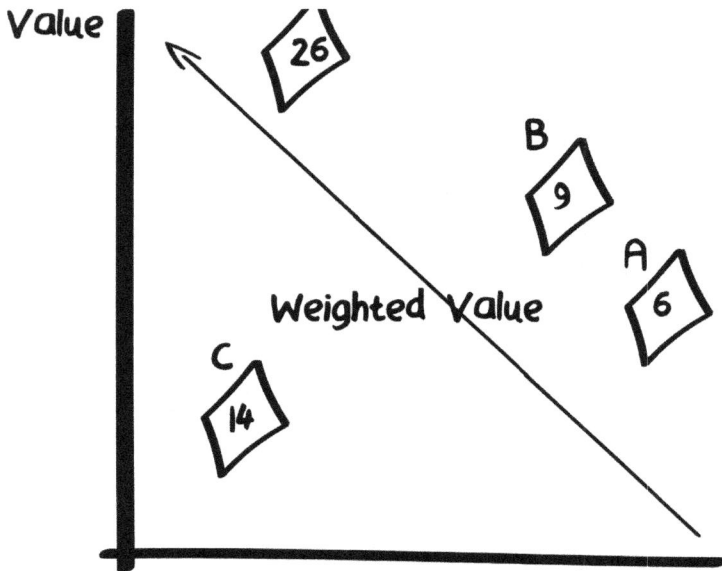

Value

26

B
9

A
6

Weighted Value

C
14

She gave each project a score and drew a line of weighted value priority up to the highest value for the lowest time.

"Based on the relative value to each other, time remaining to deliver on the project, and the estimated time available for my team, does everyone agree that Project D is the highest priority, followed by Project C?"

There were some smiles and frowns but no disagreement. She'd gotten through to them. Finally, they understood what she'd been saying. Being able to deliver one project, and maybe two, instead of partially completing all of them was the best option.

"Thanks for your time helping me resolve the prioritisation order," Julie said, gracious in victory. "It's been greatly appreciated."

Prioritising for value

"So they all agreed? Just like that?" Mark looked shocked,

almost suspicious. "Maybe if we provide a priority model, we can preempt these conversations in the future?

"Agreed" exclaimed Julie. "We need to look at it from across the organisation, I will implement it in my team so that we do not fully annoy Patrick, but if it works we should try and see if everyone else is keen to prioritise."

"From what I heard, there seem to be three stages of prioritisation," said Mark as he went over to the whiteboard.

1. Type - If it is running our business or changing it
2. Values - How we measure success at NZFS
3. Capacity - Maximising utilisation of people

"Correct, running the business is sometimes referred to as Business As Usual (BAU) or maintenance. Anything that is serving current customers is more important, normally than anything new, I would also add continuous improvement as reducing our run cost should be a high ROI."

"So, is this just CAPEX?" Mark was referring to project capital or CAPEX, a way of segmenting costs between capital assets and operational costs (OPEX).

"I don't think we need to worry about the taxation rules for this. Work is work. There are only so many hours in the day to answer emails, code, test and have lunch.

We need to put ALL work through the funnel, making it a single list of things to do, or as some would call it, a single backlog to rule them all."

"Alright, Gandalf " laughed Mark. Again Julie did not, so Mark just sipped on his coffee and went back to the whiteboard.

Julie continued, "all maintenance is ring-fenced to avoid capacity issues or risk of priority one issues. For my team that's 60% currently. For the next financial year, we should also ring fence off 10% more for continuous improvement, I am not comfortable with that 60% run cost, it limits our potential. This leaves 30% capacity for changing the business."

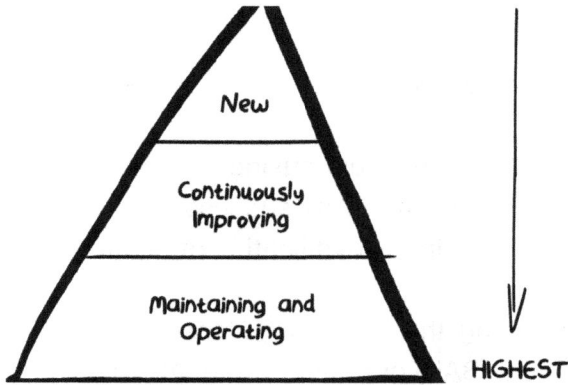

"Then we need some form of way of measuring value. I was able to get away with relative value this time, but if this is to scale, it needs to be objective. NZFS only cares about profit right now, so we will have to ensure all projects are linked back to financial gain. I am concerned with finances because it's data that lags; we have a lot of projects that estimate millions of dollars in revenue, but how often do we see it?"

"Hardly ever, if it was true, our companies' industry average profit would increase" Mark smirks as he has seen NZFS fall behind the competitors, he isn't wrong about the industry. All our profits have increased, this always happens in a property boom, but we have fallen behind our local competitors and to be honest, if the property Market were to tank, I wonder if we would survive.

Mark drew on the whiteboard some ideas "For now we will stick to financials, but we should look at KPIs that are leading the way, then weigh those against the projects in the future. We need to think about reducing costs, like our run cost, and increasing customer satisfaction and sustainability. Customer Value needs to be holistic, not just profit."

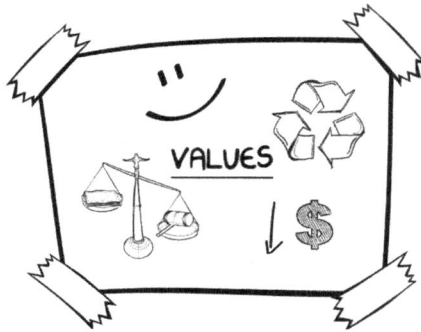

"Agreed" proclaimed Julie. "Lastly we need to think about the capacity. If we don't take capacity into the equation, we might prioritise projects which are awesome but have constraints on teams or individuals. We need to know:

- What skills are required for each project
- Each teams capacity for change
- We need to relative size the project and look at dependencies

This will allow us to re-prioritise for maximum utilisation. It would also change project behaviour"

"I don't understand how" said Mark

"It will mean a few things. To be prioritised to be worked on, you must have a benefit realisation plan, you must have a stakeholder matrix and you need to have talked to the teams prior to showing the project. Yet this will only get you on the list, projects will need to be smaller to ensure high enough ROI to be prioritised AND not have capacity issues. We don't want to get into a situation where a single team is needed for everything and becomes a constraint"

"I am sure Patrick will be very happy, are you going to roll this out with your team first?"

"Absolutely, we have an iteration one going for the rest of the year but I will send this drawing out to the others in our team to show them from next year, we will only be taking one item at a time. I am sure that will go down well.

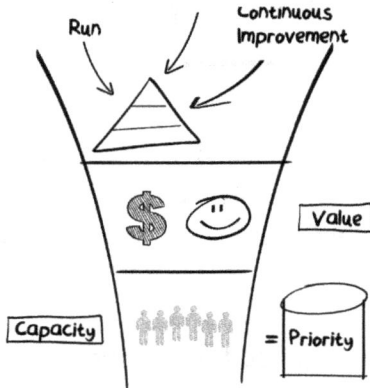

Strategic Agility Measurements

Mark's eyes lit up, he grabbed a spare whiteboard. "The strategic agility paper I read this morning was focussed on three key areas, right?

Vision - the ability for everything to be linked from an organisation why to the value of a knowledge worker

Emergent - how an organisation's strategy allows itself to change direction based on data

Pivoting - In what way an organisation changes between deliverables

What you have demonstrated right now, is moving from efficient project management where all time is utilised to productive outcome delivery of the highest value first!"

"Absolutely Mark" Julie looked like a light bulb had jumped on.

Mark continued, "So if we use your distinctions between magenta to green, we should be able to build a simple yes/no answer to each principle. This means we might have four values and if we have three per value, we would have twelve principles, or put simply twelve questions to ask ourselves `what is our current state?'

Julie started drawing a linear best to worst case scenario with each principle of strategic agility.

Mark ensured that Green was always people-centric, and that the benefits would be innovation. Orange was always outcome focused, the benefits would be productivity, Amber was structure and uniformity, with benefits of efficiency, Red was control driven which would only benefit a reactive environment and magenta was the worst-case scenario.

Vision
Organisations with one clear vision allow greater strategic alignment and network

Magenta: There is no Strategic Vision

Red: There is a Strategic Vision for management but no clear connection between work and vision

Amber: One Strategic Vision for all to see and work towards

Orange: Organisation has input into shaping the Strategic Vision;

work and vision are connected

Green: Strategic Vision is driven by the customer and teams use this to drive decision

---

Pivot

To allow the organisation to pivot with new information from the market

Magenta: There is no strategy

Red: Strategy is created every 3-5 years by executives

Amber: Goals are set every 3-5 years with a yearly strategy based on value

Orange: 30-120 day strategy plans are being used with a single prioritised backlog based on value

Green: The strategy is that there is no strategy. Everyone adds to the single backlog and the most valuable work is completed first

---

Emergent

Rapid testing of a hypothesis leads to greater innovation and re-planning

Magenta: The strong fight for budget

Red: Management raises business cases based on budget

Amber: Business cases are raised for yearly budget approval with ROI

Orange: Lean business canvas or similar are produced and approved within a financial quarter, with either a focus on competition or value metric

Green: Hypothesis testing is completed to validate the highest priority every month. Internal disruption is promoted

Ok, so let's do it now, here at NZFS we have a vision set from the top, and we are technically all working towards it, the big four help set up strategic goals every three years and then we raise strategic initiatives yearly. So we are Amber?"

Now Julie was happy, "not quite Mark, you are absolutely correct that we have yearly strategic initiatives, but they are not based on value as we have no measure of value or concrete benefit realisation, as a friend once told me, you can't be half pregnant. So we take a step back to red on Pivot. To be amber we would need to prioritise our yearly strategy"

Mark and Julie looked at the strategic agility value and three principles and it did resemble their world. There was a vision but managers were the ones that decided what was done, but not based on objectivity and we approve business cases prior to the financial year. Mostly amber, we work towards efficiency, but it was a form of paternalistic authority that the managers knew best. The elephant in the room was red under pivot. It showed a highly reactive environment which was unlikely to be an advantage.

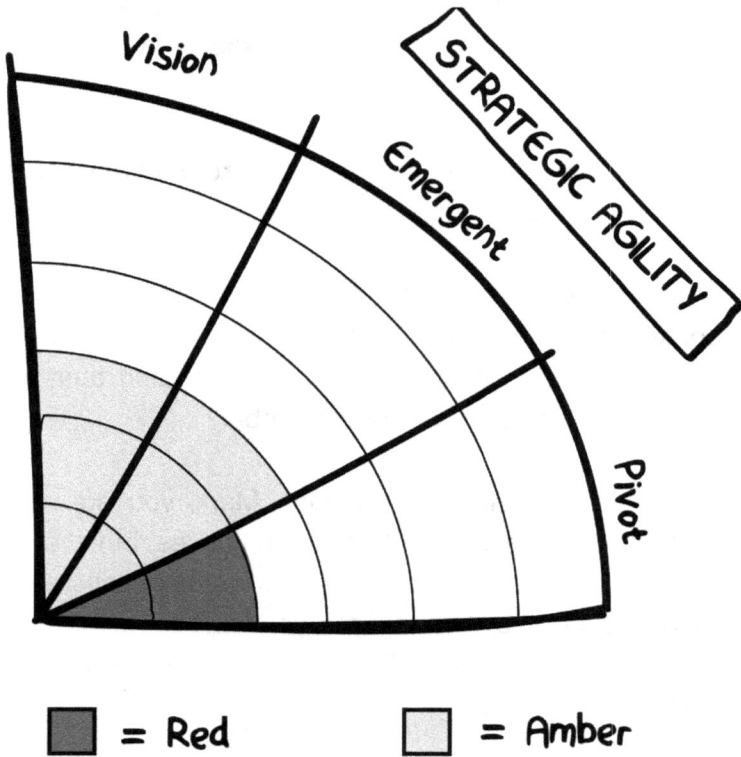

STRATEGIC AGILITY

Vision — Emergent — Pivot

■ = Red   □ = Amber

"If we implement your changes to priority?" Mark said while jumping to his feet. "Yes, then we would be Amber for Strategic Agility", "So where do we start?" Mark said with a smile.

"We start where we are, we must finish the current state analysis first but I suspect we need to bring that pivot up to Amber first so we do not have an unstable culture before moving Strategic Agility to Orange. Next, we need to agree and evaluate the diversity of getting work done, aka cognitive diversity. Here is tonight's homework" Julie's hands Mark a printed copy of "Cognitive Diversity for High Performance. "

Cognitive Diversity

Customer-centric structure

The drive for customer-centric structures is based on the need to obtain dynamic capabilities. In this paper, we look at the definition of customer-centric structures and how they can be implemented. Dynamic capabilities are linked to greater financial performance[9], and understanding missed opportunities[10].

Dynamic capabilities are defined as "the firm's ability to integrate, build, and reconfigure internal and external competences to address rapidly changing environments[11]".

To obtain dynamic capabilities, Lee and Day created a framework for a customer-centric structure that gives hypothetical dynamic capabilities to adapt to new requirements[12]. Day in 2011 described the importance of a fluid Marketing organisation that anticipates and adapts to new customer demands, allowing rapid prototyping of new initiatives for customers.

Customer-Centric Structure is defined as:

"Structural design in which a firm's business units are aligned with distinct customer groups, rather than product groups"
(Lee & Day, 2018)

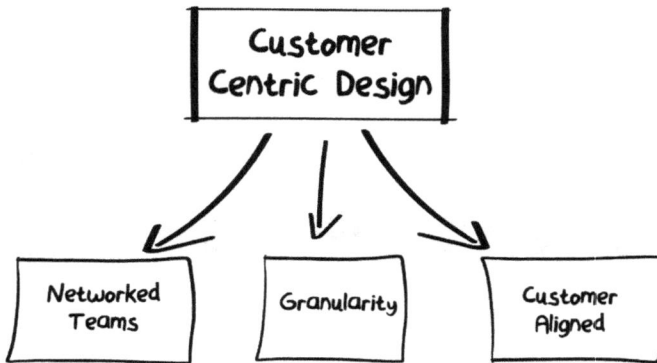

Lee & Day focus on aligning each business unit with a single customer segmentation, networking teams for cross-functional delivery and more granularity to decrease the number of steps from value creators and customers.. With additional alignment with the customer, it allows organisations to shift quickly on new information, aligns to customer insights sooner by identifying shifts in their chosen customer segmentation. Greater accountability for teams to serve the customer ensures dynamic capabilities[13].

Porter describes in a Harvard business review webinar that companies will need to create structures that give closer relationships with the customer if they want to keep their competitive advantage[14].

Disaggregating business units into smaller sizes increases agility. Tribes can be between 25-150[15], at the higher end of 150, our neuro capability to form relations causes a decrease in agility, however, this high number is designed to be short-lived in extreme environments.

Logan and Dunbar's research does not take into consideration the reduction in employee loyalty and the increased connectivity of today's social world. The number for a tribe would be lower than it would be in the 1990s and substantially lower in cultures where empowerment is normal. There is a downside to smaller sized units, coordination costs increase, making the positive impact of customer satisfaction mute[16].

Leveraging from the work of Arons, Driest and Weed on the Orchestrator model, Lee and Day stress the importance of a network from the grass-root level. Lee & Day articulate the need for customer-centric design.

Employees required this network to be transparent to one another, with the ability to "own" their work, as opposed to management owning it for them. The factors that prohibit innovation and dynamic capabilities are having the right skills closer to the customers.

Cognitive diversity is defined as the needed capabilities within the structure to release the potential of the organisation. Without cognitive diversity, an organisations competitive advantage is diminished through waste in the value chain, bureaucracy and a culture that does not adapt fast enough for the customers needs. Structuring an organisation around the end to end value delivered to the customer enables lowered time to Market, increased customer satisfaction and reduced cost of deployment of value. Key factors for delivering cognitive diversity within a value chain is in the ability for a value chain to pivot, thus the transparency of knowledge can be a barrier to entry for some organisations, however, organisations can not just force the change with structure and transparency, the people in the organisation must feel safe and motivated to make decisions without fear of punishment or judgement; the organisations mindset needs to be focused on change for tomorrow and not on static for today.

Value chain Analysis

Julie dragged her feet coming into the office, it had only been four weeks but had felt like four months this autumn Monday morning. The motivation was gone and she felt as though her job was now a continuous fight to keep up with, there was no time for change.

As she went up the escalators to the Auckland offices, Mark's face slowly appeared as if he was waiting for someone. Why was he so happy? Maybe I should go vegan, she thought.

"Julie! I've been waiting, you're late!" Julie took a glance at her phone, 8:24am and frowned, "no, we have nothing booked, you are just normally here at 8", Mark smiled. "Your first meeting is at 9, so follow me".

Julie thought about walking the opposite way but decided to follow Mark, maybe his fun vibe will rub off. Mark led her to a room on level 15 that was labelled as THE WAR ROOM, which Julie noted another violent set of labelling that needs to change.

"So I read your document on cognitive diversity and it clicked for me, we have been structured in such a way that we don't even know how value is truly delivered, this will always prohibit us from being productive. We don't have the right organisational mindset for how we change, you yourself mentioned how one of your Business Analysts was PUT ON training as opposed to her finding the right solution and finally to achieve cognitive diversity, we would need to be transparent with our information. This room took me all weekend to complete because everything was hidden on many variations of documented management systems."

It was at this moment Julie remembered she gave the cognitive diversity paper to Mark last week and then as if by magic, or her flat white kicking in, she saw the room was covered in flow diagrams that looked like value chains.

A value chain is a way of looking at the different activities that a company does to create value for its customers. It helps businesses identify which activities are most important to their success and where they can improve.

Agile value chains are becoming more popular as businesses strive to be more agile and responsive to change. An agile value chain is one that can quickly adapt to changes in the Market or business environment.

To do a value chain analysis, Mark must have audited all the different activities the company does and has identified which ones create value for customers. Julie smiled finally, "we will need to assess how well NZFS is doing at each of these activities and identify areas where they could improve, but this is amazing Mark, I can clearly see our value chains!"

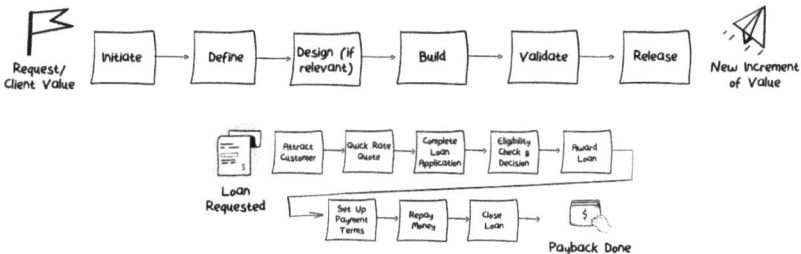

Over the next few days Mark and Julie brought in members of their teams to finalise details, as Julie said "we are not the masters of this information, it'll be the people doing the work that understand it most". It was Thursday afternoon when Simon messaged Julie on their internal messaging service

Right hand, left hand

Simon: We have an issue...

That's great; just when I thought I would have a week without an issue! Julie thought to herself

Julie: How can I be of service?

Simon: We have found a security threat; one of the developers could access private customer data from a query

Julie: OMG. Can we confirm it's only our internal staff who can access this information?

Simon: We don't know anything, to be honest, we had four incompetent contractors last year install some APIs to pull customer data from our business app to our retail app, but we don't know where this data is coming from or how big the problem is.

Julie: Did you try ringing the developers to ask them how they created the link?

Simon: Yes, they are not answering, apparently, they have new engagements now and can't help till four months' time.

Typical; Simon is blaming the contractors but it's our fault for outsourcing this development to them in the first place! Julie steamed to herself; she had seen this all over projects in her last four weeks. Development is completed by contractors and project teams; and then thrown over to her team to "operationalise" and yet there is no one who knows enough about it, to actually help. Yet I am told I am not being Agile enough by contract Agile Coaches. Oh, so Agile is running Scrum to create a product and then leaving? Sounds like a hoot.

Simon: We are in the war room, if you want to help?

Julie: Be there soon.

Julie arrives to see the War Room with Simon and Darren and George, George was one of our senior integration developers.

"Ok, what do we know?" Julie blurted out, without reading the room.

"Hi Julie, it's not good, we don't know why the data is in the clear (tech speak for not encrypted), we don't know why these data-bases are even connected and if we were to stop it, we don't know what it would stop for the customer!" Simon didn't seem happy, that's for sure.

"It's worse than that" George said sheepishly, "we are having problems following the data back to source and downstream, I built this initially for the business banking app project but the way it looks now, I don't even recognise it"

Darren laughed "but! We know it's just an internal issue. No one outside our network can access, so it's only a P3 and we can leave George to it"

"Priority 3 Darren! This is a major screw up of the project, a screw up, my team now has to fix"

Darren opened his mouth to say something when Julie blurted out... "oh no, you own this, this time. Your project, your contractors, your testing. You then threw it over the fence to my guys, expecting no problems? HA! This is EXACTLY what happens when you have separate development and operations. If you are not enjoying the lawns, you won't cut them as well as the person who does!"

Terrible analogy Julie thought, but it got her point across, Darren left nodding and saying "P3" as if this was no longer worth his time.

"Simon, what do you propose?" Julie asked in the nicest way possible.

"To be honest, to be left alone, this may take me a few days"

"I'll be back in an hour Simon, have a coffee. We are about to have fun" Julie left the room smiling.

Swarming

Julie started storming back upstairs to Mark, Simon as our tech lead seems to be the only person handling every priority, which is worrying for two reasons

1. What if Simon leaves or gets burnt out
2. Creating a single point of failure reduces performance

The fact is Simon isn't the only person in this value chain and by himself will only create one type of solution.

"Mark! I need people" Julie was storming up Mark which made Mark very uncomfortable.

"Wh... who?" said Mark, trying to get his words out

Pointing to the retail mobile app value chain "One person from each of these steps and I want them now, not tomorrow, not later, I want them dropping what they are doing now and meeting me in the war room"

"That may be difficult." Mark said

Julie sat down and started typing up an email to every team in the value chain, including marketing, sales and operations; copying in their managers separately, the CIO and CISO.

TITLE: P1 CUSTOMER DATA BREACH

Kia Ora,

Your teams have been identified as giving value from our databases to our retail mobile application.

Right now anyone within our organisation can now read customers private data via unencrypted API.

I have one lead engineer looking at this in the war room, however, as he did not write the code, this may take days to figure out. Leaving us at risk of compliance and audit violations.

I require one person from EVERY team on this mailing list to meet me in the war room in one hour for the rest of the day. It is only important that we receive one person who has capacity from each team, please talk among yourself to see who has capacity.

Yours Sincerely,

Julie

'Did you really just do that? ' Mark said, looking shocked. "I mean yes, my people have already messaged me and sent two people to help, but the other departments are outside our control.

"We will now see who cares about their customers' data, it's not what we can control but showing what matters in our realm of influence" Julie looked stern as she said it.

Julie's Phone rings. It's Greg.

"Hi Gr" Julie tried to say

"WHAT are you doing! You have just made us look completely incompetent to people outside of IT! Greg was obviously upset that this issue was raised 'externally'.

"Greg, we need everyone who touches this process, we can not solve this with just Simon. It requires knowledge that my team does not hold, do you want this P1 fixed today?"

"Of Course I do Julie, however, you have just created an auditable trail, I had Alex the CISO on the phone saying now! we can't ignore your issue. This isn't how you make friends" Greg seemed to be calming down

"I am not here to make friends Greg, I am here for our customers, now I need to lead this P1 crisis, have a wonderful day" Julie put the phone down as politely as she could.

"Let's go Mark, I've left Simon alone for 30 minutes and knowing him he hasn't even got a coffee yet.

Julie went to the local cafe and picked up two double shot flat whites and a long black for Simon, Mark and herself and ordered some snacks to be delivered. "How many people" the lovely cafe lady asks. Laughing to herself, "let's say six people, please".

As Julie went up the escalator towards the ground floor, there seemed to be a lot of people moving furniture, blocking her path. Which intuitively annoyed Julie, it was slowing her down further.

"JULIE!' Simon was glowing.

"Here is your coffee Simon" Julie tried to smile back

"Did you do this? Look? We have over thirty people turn up from all over the business, we are moving furniture to the board room to fit everyone. They all want to help! I don't even know who half these people are!"

Julie suddenly looked gobsmacked and struggled to say anything, as she watched engineers, sales, marketing, operations, security and even people & culture walking towards the boardroom, she heard plenty of conversations about 'finally not being left out', 'help the customer' and 'poor Simon all alone in that room with no coffee'.

Julie quickly rang the Cafe to ask for enough sausage rolls for 30 people and that coffee orders will be coming soon.

Crowd Power
"Kia Ora Koutou Everyone, I am excited, privileged and honoured that you have all come to solve this P1. Somewhere in our product journey there has been an issue, how it was caused is not a

concern for us. Our focus is now how do we resolve this as quickly as possible. I want to build the value chain properly from start to finish and align how we all give value to this journey. Then I want to test each section to see if we can find this breach in security, how does that sound?" Julie saw a room full of excited people nod to say go ahead. To concrete the reason they are all here, Julie remembered a story.

"Sir Francis Galton was at a country fair in 1906 where he came across a competition to guess the weight of an Ox, the results were astonishing, 787 guesses with an average of 1'197 pounds were calculated with the actual weight being 1'198 pounds. The power of the crowd was even more accurate then the experts at the time. That was 1906 and I have always been suspicious. However, in 2018 Penelope the cow was an online survey with over 3500 respondents, you can see by the results, that not only did crowd power work recently but the experts which were fewer in numbers, were farther off. I know, with the people we have here, we will accurately diagnose the problem and solve it quicker and better than If we had one expert on the case " Julie opened the hui which received a lot of happy faces and compliments.

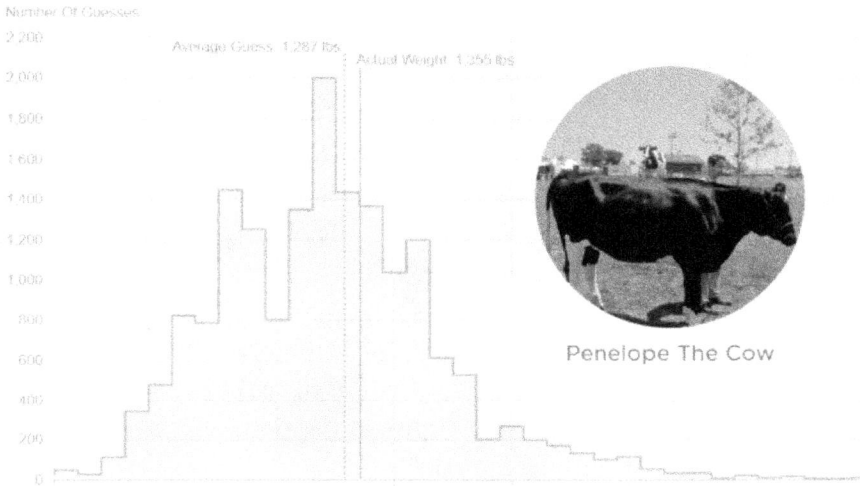

Number Of Guesses

2,200
2,000
1,800
1,600
1,400
1,200
1,000
800
600
400
200
0

Average Guess 1,287 lbs   Actual Weight 1,355 lbs

Penelope The Cow

(Experts Only)

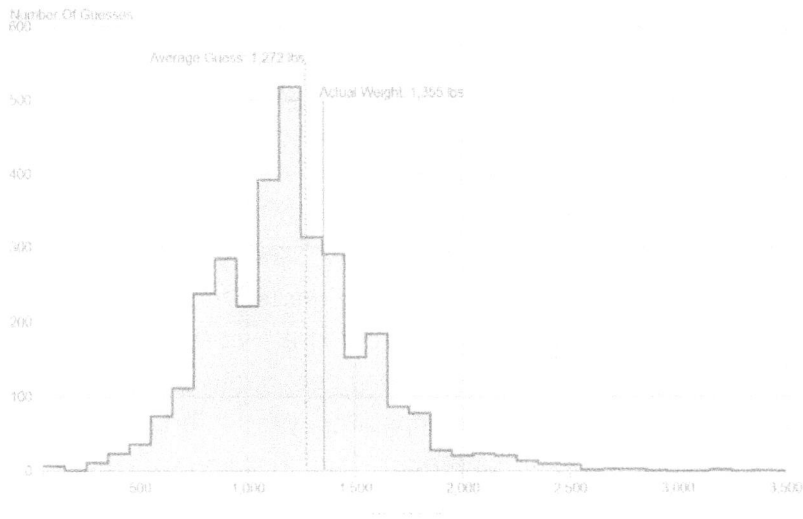

Number Of Guesses
600

Average Guess 1,272 lbs

500

400

300

200

100

0

Actual Weight 1,355 lbs

500   1,000   1,500   2,000   2,500   3,000   3,500

For two hours the 'team' worked together mapping out a very complex product value chain, one that was far more detailed than what Mark and Julie had done. Scenarios and people they hadn't even realised were part of the value chain. The retail value chain included 247 people!

"What this is showing them all Julie, is that without each other, there is no actual value. I have never seen departments come together so well. The empathy is amazing to watch" Mark said, looking astonished.

"Thank you all." Simon was suddenly standing on a chair "I can not believe we have not only reset our processes, realised new pains that each other has caused each other inadvertently, but more importantly, we have found the issue in the data. I have turned off the connection to the report that exposed the data, our customers data is now secure. Thank you again"

As everyone congratulated themselves and started leaving, Julie got many requests to do this again as it was fun, which shocked Julie.

"So what was the issue?" Julie asked Simon once everyone had gone.

"It wasn't Darren's project, we were barking up the wrong tree there. It was People and Culture who triggered me to look at something. The leadership team had created a report outside of IT to get data, and they worked around the security to get the data they needed. I can't tell you which consultancy did it, but it'll be one of them that was able to get around the security. I guess if you tap on enough shoulders with the backing of the CIO, you can do anything.

If we hadn't banded together like this, I would have likely not found this issue and then created a work around, leaving more technical debt. Thank you Julie. I am going to go back now to my P3s and project work" Simon left smiling, leaving Julie sitting in a boardroom that looked like kids had been playing in there.

Julie went back to her desk and requested the laptop from her predecessor. After looking through their documents, Julie found what she was looking for. Documentation on why this was done and a reminder to patch it after. Looking upset that the answer was right here, all along, Julie called greg.

"The p1 has been resolved"

"I heard, well done. I hear our management report may be changing as well" Greg said almost smugly.

"Yes, what is worse is that the documents are on the old GMs laptop and probably yours as well. We need to move all local files to a central system. We have a technology system that creates all our work in one place but we also need the organisations document management and workflows all in one place. We have started creating the value chains and I recommend we carry on and store them in this way. No more local storage." Julie calmly laid out her information.

"Sure, add it to the business plan coming up next month, sounds reasonable" Greg put the phone down, I am sure in a polite way.

Be Agile, don't do Agile
Julie thought she could relax, so went downstairs to level 8 to see her team.

"No! I will not agree to have it done by the end of the day" Susan was almost shouting at Simon

"But you said you would have the document finished by yesterday" Simon looked frustrated, which wasn't like him.
"I said I would try, I didn't say I would" huffed Susan.

"Ok, how can I help, walk me through it?" Julie thought she would try and help. Simon and Susan portrayed their versions of events, which sounded more like kids playing with he said, she said.

"When new work comes in and we break it down into our sprints, do we not all agree on priority and rough duration?"

"Absolutely not" Susans tone took Julie back, "A lot of our requirements documents, which this team now splits into user stories, user stories are these small conversational points with a fictitious person, a goal to achieve and the benefit we want to achieve. Sounds great in theory, until you realise our person is always in another department, not the user or customer, the requirements are far too complex to give a timeframe and the quality of using user stories means either I spend twice as long doing the analysis, or I get questions and issues for it, while I am trying to write the next ones!"

Julie remembered her Agile Training in her last job. She wasn't a fan of the Agile Coach harping on, everything sounded good in theory until the practicals, which seemed more like demands then recommendations. The User Story was one of them. The idea of a user story was to "start a conversation", it wasn't designed to cause this level of stress for the team.

```
* AS A <role>
* I WANT <goal>
* SO THAT <benefit>

Acceptance Criteria:
(Conditions of Satisfaction)
```

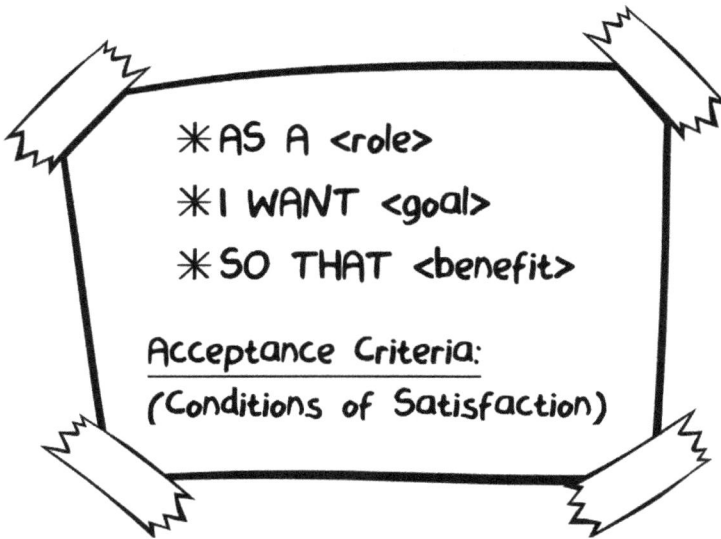

"The sprints you mention, this time boxed duration for delivery for our supposed Scrum framework? Is nothing more than the last GMs way of trying to speed us up. He introduced Scrum with all these promises of a better working environment, but all I seem to be doing is delivering poor quality documentation and being rushed to complete more, then when something goes wrong... I AM to blame again."

"I had no idea" Simon looked hurt, "I thought user stories and sprints helped you and Darren, the developers hate them as well. Every two weeks we pretend we can achieve what Darren wants, even though we know we won't, the user stories are worthless to us because we need to know the entire end to end, if we don't know the outcome, we will continuously make assumptions and then we get issues."

"Well this seems like a simple solution." Julie said with a smile. "Stop using user stories and stop doing Scrum."

The pause made everyone uncomfortable, it seemed that not using Scrum was an issue. Scrum is a lightweight delivery framework for complex products. It doesn't have many rules Julie thought, but it also does come with baggage. It normally ends up being implemented the same way. An expensive consultant is invited in from the GM, who sets up two week "sprints", moves the projects into a single list of work called a "product backlog", where at the start of the two week period, the team will agree to complete a Scrum Goal by the end of the two weeks, meets daily to discuss issues (Daily Scrum) and then show the owner of the work, normally called the product owner and then they reflect on how to do things better in the next sprint. It's meant to be sustainable and the team's choice.

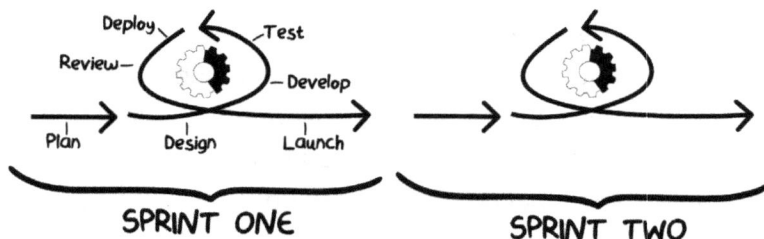

Adapted from Scrum.Org

"Julie, if we are not agile, we won't meet our key performance indicators"

"First of all, using Scrum as a framework doesn't make you Agile and second, Agile Delivery is merely one way of delivering outcomes. Our team has no scrum masters, no product owners, high maintenance costs, we do not deliver the outcome by ourselves and we are driven by project budget. I am surprised these conversations haven't come up in your Sprint Retrospective?"

Simon looked towards the coffee machine before answering, "I think this is the first time any of us have raised these issues, Darrens has done the best job he can as our de facto Scrum Master, but his main job IS project manager. In our developer catch ups, we always say to each other this isn't working but we always thought the others were happy, the organisation measures us on our acceptance of agile and I guess, we thought this was the way things are done here now."

Five Dysfunctions of a team

"Hogwash, if this isn't working for you, change it. You mentioned to me on day one, that you were one big team. However, you are clearly separating functions, both of you" Julie looked at Susan who clearly wanted to leave the conversation now. "Patrick Lencioni in his book "5 Dysfunctions of a team" talks about how artificial harmony in a team is caused by an absence of trust.

I am glad however, you have had this conflict as now we can resolve it. I want you to book a session with all 30 of your TEAM next week. We will all reflect together, not a Scrum Retrospective, we will use Bassots reflection to take from the past actions into the future to fix these issues. As for the KPIs, please ignore them, I want you to find a way to help each other that delivers customer outcomes, I do not care for how many sprints you do"[17]

"Thank you Julie" Susan and Simon looked like a weight had been lifted from around their neck.

As Simon left, Susan asked "you said 5, but mentioned one?"

Any chance Julie has to grab a white board is a positive she thought, "yes, to create a cohesive team, Patrick mentions there are five things to overcome. Although there is a lot of fun research in team dynamics as a topic, this one is quite easy to remember. The first dysfunction of a team is Trust.

Teams must be open or vulnerable with each other, without trust you can not have a team because without trust you can not have good conflict, it causes an invulnerability outcome, where everything seems to be great from the outside.

Healthy conflict is needed on a team, it allows teams to find the truth without the fear of being judged, which is the second dysfunction. Without healthy conflict, there is artificial harmony. Having open and honest conversations allows you to overcome the third dysfunction, lack of commitment; teams who are passive in their decision making have results that are ambiguous.

Commitment means everyone buys in, which allows a team to avoid the fourth; avoidance of accountability, this one is very common, if we don't commit, we can't hold each other accountable and therefore we end up with low standards in what we do.

If a team can hold each other accountable it helps us avoid the fifth dysfunction; inattention to results, teams can often focus on their own ego and status when they don't focus on the results of the team."

"Wow, so because you saw that the conflict we had wasn't healthy, you were able to identify we had artificial harmony, caused by a lack of trust?"

"Correct, now we can solve this issue by ensuring everyone knows they can choose a way of working that delivers results that matter to NZFS, if we all trust each other, then conflict will become normal and fun."

"Awesome, I look forward to our retro…. I mean reflection."

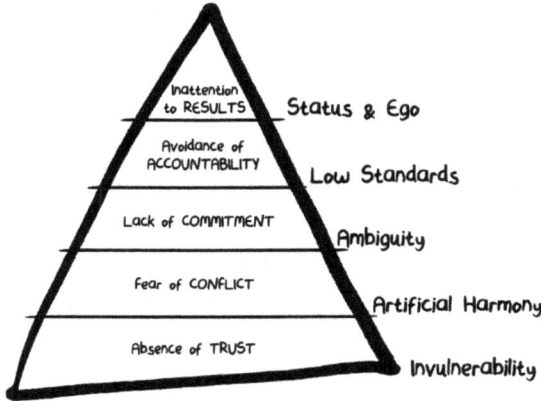

Adapted from The Five Dysfunctions of a Team | Patrick Lencioni

~

"It's 5:34pm Mark, do we have to do this now?"

"Yes, come on, strike while the iron is hot!"

Cognitive Diversity Measures

Mark continued "I've been working on this all afternoon, so it'll be quick. Cognitive diversity is the ability to have all the right people surrounding a problem, it is just as much about the people themselves as it is about the leadership and the structure of an organisation. So I was thinking that our three measurements for cognitive diversity should be our people's Mindset, but more about how that mindset is enabled by leadership, organisations that focus on a growth mindset around the customer will be people centric, however, those that focus on themselves will be more centralised.

Our value chain and how we are either structured around

efficiency, outcome or the customer. We know from our conversations that an organisation that is customer focused will reduce the number of people between the customer and the person doing the work, however, those that focus on just getting the work done, will split the people over multiple value chains and look for efficiencies in the process.

Lastly, how transparent the organisation is with its knowledge, people and process. Organisations that truely want to serve the customer, need fast acting information that enables continuous improvements, as opposed to those organisations that centralise authority and documentation to serve their departments best interests."

"Honestly, I am starting to wonder if I would have completed this without you Mark, thank you" Julie started to read the stages one by one on the whiteboard.

Mindset
How our people learn will enable organisational growth at a cultural level

Magenta: What's wrong with a fixed mindset?

Red: If we want to improve, we need new people

Amber: Prescribed feedback is given to individuals and training courses are booked

Orange: Feedback loops allow individuals to learn and continuous development without management approval (online e-courses)

Green: Teams are responsible for continuous learning and

teaching new members of the team and a growth mindset is embedded into our culture

---

Value chain
How an organisation is structured will increase costs or deliver greater business outcomes in specific environments

Magenta: No deliberate strategy for employees

Red: Organisation is mapped based on functional silos with no map to customer value

Amber: Teams are aligned to functional silos within multiple value chains. Some may have virtual teams aligned with the customer value

Orange: Teams work within functional silos within single value chain and/or no customer has been engaged

Green: Teams are cross functional within a single value chain and are aligned to the customer view of value

---

Transparency
Organisations that are more transparent and open, ensure their people have the knowledge they need to make critical decisions.

Magenta: I am unsure where the knowledge is kept

Red: Knowledge is available on management computers

Amber: Organisation knowledge is communicated and stored

centrally

Orange: Information is freely available to read but admin is an individual

Green: Knowledge is openly promoted and discussed for all to update - Wikipedia

"I agree, these are great Mark, they align nicely with the values and the stages of culture that represent Magenta to Green.

When I first arrived, I noticed that training was literally booked FOR people and today we observed that ways of working are done to them. We don't just get new people when there is a problem but we also don't have an environment where they can continuously learn by themselves. Amber?"

"I agree Julie, Amber for Mindset, I was thinking of Amber for Value chains as well. We do have customer value chains, however, everyone is in functional silos, working across multiple customer segmentations. We saw that today when we had our P1."

"That makes sense, Transparency... we clearly saw today that management has centralised knowledge. Red. Great, now I am off home"

Julie looks at her watch, 6:20pm, maybe she can tuck her kids in tonight, instead of Granddad doing it, at least it's Thursday, it's a holiday tomorrow, which means a three day weekend. Maybe I can get the kids up to look at the stars tomorrow?

"Are you not forgetting something?"

"Now what Mark!?"

"I need my homework for the weekend"

"It's a New Zealand holiday tomorrow, I'll email you customer experience now, but with a time delay. You will receive it Saturday; Ngā mihi.

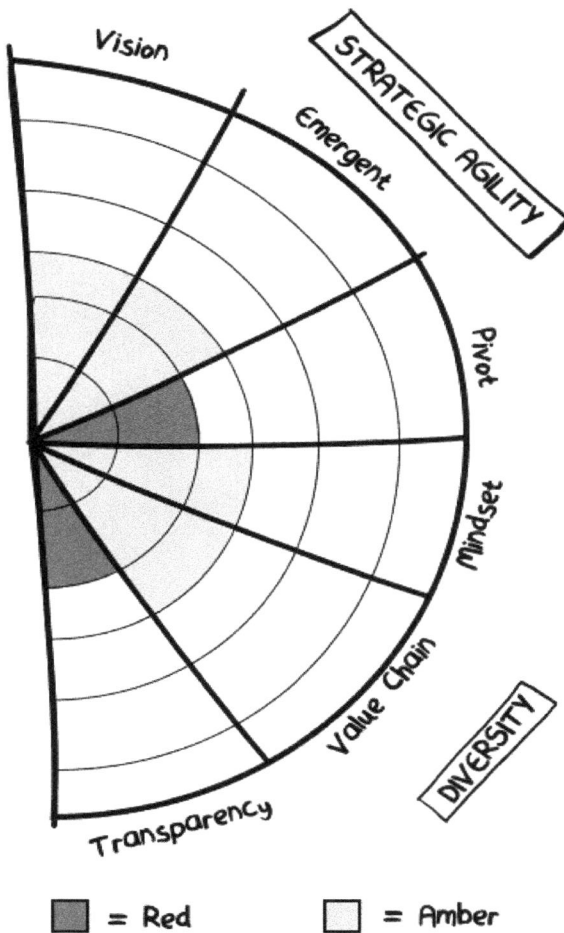

Vision
Emergent
STRATEGIC AGILITY
Pivot
Mindset
Value Chain
DIVERSITY
Transparency

▓ = Red   ☐ = Amber

Agility Matters

Customer Experience

Importance of Customer Experience

Customers can be involved in the organisation at various stages, this study looks at how customer involvement in product development impacts customer value.

Vision and strategy start from the board of directors. Customer involvement in setting strategy, creating a vision and holding the chief executive accountable is more effective for an organisation when they are more diverse[18].

Bommaraju et al. found in their analysis of 329 business to business firms, that having a customer on the board had a medium correlation of 0.331 with firms performance. However, when markets are complex, this becomes a moderate correlation of 0.527, arguing that a customer on the board can be at least as important as a Marketing executive on the board (2019). Business to business studies would normally not be fit for purpose, however, it is relevant to this study as the board members did not have more than 10% of the customer base and would not have bias towards their own company, much like a "customer of a business" to "customer organisation" would have limited reward for board choices.

Having customer involvement at the strategic level can ensure a true customer view is taken into account, this can help the customer value increase by focusing on social and/or emotional value directly. Corporate social responsibility (CSR) is an example of customer demand where customer involvement can shape the board towards social value which may be more aligned to what the customers want to see organisations achieve.

Innovation leads to financial performance and research shows that only 25% of new products are successful in the market[19]. Accessing the success factors of innovation allows organisations to focus on what is most likely to succeed in the market.

Evanschitzky, Eisend, Calantone, and Jiang updated Henard and Szymanski meta-analysis for product success, taking results up to 2012, allowing today's culture to be included. Customer input into the new product development was a weak correlation of 0.21, however, greater than technology superiority (0.06). Of this meta-analysis, a weak correlation of 0.21 was the highest recorded; customer input and reduced cycle times shine a light on getting the product into the hands of the customer and validating a hypothesis quicker[20]. There was no evidence that the meta-analysis only measured customer involvement where a company was already structured around the customer, this leads this author to believe that the majority of the negative correlation was with targeting the wrong customer and the customer not being able to adequately influence change in the organisation, thus reducing the effectiveness of the customer involvement. It is worth noting that Szymanski and Henard found a correlation of 0.41 with customer input against product success, all of Syzmanski and Henard results were higher correlated to success than Evanschitzky et al. (2001); Evanschitzky et al. suspected this was due to cultural changes and how the Market is more complex, which may mean new ways of measuring are required. (2012).

Saldanha, Mithas and Krishnan found that it is vital to have customer involvement for achieving outcomes (2017). Information technology departments must continuously innovate to keep or grow their competitive advantage. Collaborating with customers isn't enough, the customer must be involved as part of the team from start to finish, to increase performance and innovation[21]. Saldanha et al. found a weak correlation between product customer involvement and innovation (0.10). However, found a moderate negative correlation with innovation having information-intensive customer involvement (-0.32).

When involving a customer, merely focusing on surveys or limited contact with customers isn't enough to increase innovation and company performance. More in-depth involvement, like being on the team, helps to build relationships, Li et al. found that building customer relationships increased performance of an organisation by increasing trust and commitment[22].

Product development can benefit from cross-functional design. The cross-functional design includes the customer, by bringing the customer along the journey, the brand loyalty increase allows customers to moderate the impact of a poor performing product[23].

Stephan Lagrosen argues that there are four main areas of involvement the customer can be in for product development (2005):
- Idea Generation - Brainstorming etc
- Product Optimisation - Concept testing etc
- Marketing Mix - Simulation testing etc

- Prediction - analysis etc

Cross-functional teams, including the customer, were found to mitigate the risk of the customer viewpoints being neglected. Benefits were found across all four stages, specifically in the sales at the end, however, risk of producing products the customer does not want is increased without the customer involvement in idea generation. The cost was cited as the main reason not to have customers involved. Neither study looked at how the organisation's products could be used by the employees, setting up the organisation for leveraging customer involvement from within[24].

Lagrosen found that getting customer input was troublesome for organisations which also builds on "the importance of the relationship is to build together". Voice of the customer is developing a relationship with the customer, through constant interactions from start to finish of product design[25].

When developing a product, there are many points in which a customer involvement can be beneficial; board-level customer involvement in vision, product design and product development have positive impacts on the success of the product. Customer involvement increases trust and loyalty and reduces the risk of customer upset after purchase.

Customer satisfaction can be recorded throughout the vision, strategy and product development, instead of at the end of the process, mitigating any upsets. Brand loyalty increases with better customer understanding and trust. Increasing brand loyalty or customer satisfaction can be strongly correlated to re-purchase and customer championing the organisation[26], therefore cost reduction in the customer retention would be a direct result of involving the customer, increasing customer value so the net cost-benefit is less.

The limitations of these studies are in the direct customer value increases relative to costs of involving the customer. There is good documentation for involving a customer at the board level and the product level but not the cost associated, also organisations evaluated never thought to see the percentage of their employees using their products. A margin analysis would help to show the net customer value impact for changes. The research is also missing customer involvement in customer-centric structures, this would show if the increase in customer value is specific to the customer involvement, on top of the structure change.

Organisations currently focus on their product development without the customer, leading to waste. Although stakeholder engagement can help mitigate issues, this is often a tick box rather than full participation, that may not cover a lousy management decision. Some organisations use customer feedback surveys to get data from the customer. Feedback directly from customers is promoted, however, there is room for error as customers may not tell the truth, and the surveys are historical in nature[27].

Having the customer embedded into the product initiation will ensure that the customer's voice helps shape the product, transparency is delivered and the product reduces the risk of delivering features that do not solve the customer's problem, thus reducing project costs and increasing the chance of product success[28].

Customers being involved in the product initiation was a concern for organisations with expensive intellectual property, however, with the rate of change increasing, secretive approach to strategy development has run its course in favour of the greater customer experience.

Research completed on achieving strategic objectives is considerable; however, very little has connected the customer experience and strategic objectives. A company's primary focus is to create value for its customer[29]; therefore, serving that customer should mean the customer is at the heart of everything an organisation does.

Organisations should have complete alignment between strategic objectives and customer experience, and thus by focusing on more exceptional customer experiences, you would achieve more significant strategic objectives.

This study's background follows the technology and cultural changes that happened over the last hundred years and how that has led us to the current position organisations are in today. The ability to be flexible, adapt to new data and respond accordingly, is showing a strong correlation with achieving strategic objectives.

Do we talk to our customers?
Julie was enjoying her coffee, it was 5:34am, the sun was tucked away, the heat pump was on full and although central Auckland had light pollution, she could see it was a clear morning, it was going to be a great Monday.

Getting ahead of Mark this time, Julie sat and enjoyed the customer centric documentation she wrote last year and realised she had forgotten a lot of vital information. While making the kids lunches, she thought about where in the organisation there was actual customer involvement. Had she seen a true customer on the floor? There were Product Owners in Digital, did they talk to the customer? How can they represent the customer if they weren't talking to anyone?

- Two Kids Dressed
- Two Kids Lunches in bag
- Two Kids Fed

- One Kid watching TV, the other starting his walk.
- #MumLife

8:00am and Julie is almost bouncing up the street towards her offices, a Flat White on route and a quick admiration of the calm pacific ocean before taking the escalators up to the ground floor.

Interesting, no Mark. Julie went to the war room and yes, there was Mark. Julie wondered if Mark slept in the office. Mental check she thought, look for sleeping bags.

"Morning Mark"

"Morning Julie, do you know anyone that talks directly to the customer?"

Julie smiles and shakes her head.

"Shouldn't your team talk to the customer?"

"We do, every time we do a major release, we do when we are updating our personas. My concern this morning is how we are all busy creating business outcomes for next financial year and are any of us talking to the customer about it?"

He had a point, all the technology leadership team were busy creating new projects to get into the next budget, we knew they hadn't seen our value maps, therefore they wouldn't have spoken to the people in their value chain and therefore wouldn't have created connected outcomes around the customer. Although, nor had Julie either to be fair.

"I want to clarify something first, before we ask our team members. What is a customer?"

"Isn't that just obvious Mark?"

"Then tell me" Mark said with his cheeky southern grin

"A person who consumes the end value of a product or service AND who has a choice on who else they consume from"

"Ok good, we are on the same page. When I look at the projects from this year, so many of our peers use the customer in their documents, BUT! Only one project was actually FOR the customer. That went live Thursday night by the way."

"We delivered before a three day weekend? To the customer? Fun!"

"The other projects are clearly for our internal staff to reduce cost and a larger than I realised amount was for other businesses that we help."

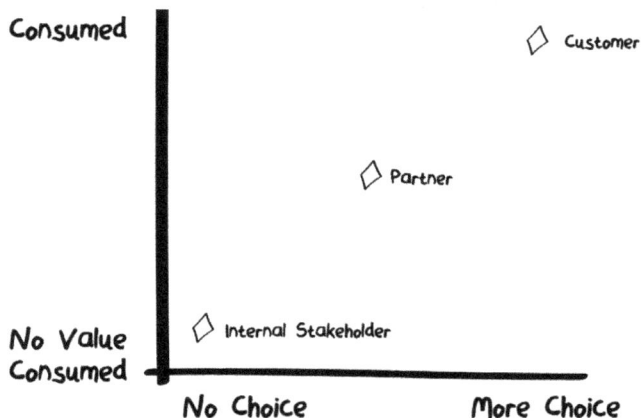

Mark drafted a chart showing value along the y axis and choice along the x axis.

"So if we map the Customer as receiving more value and having more choice, it would be a partner in our value chain who has some choice but doesn't consume the end value? Does this mean there is no such segmentation as business customers?"

"Makes sense, why would a business have business customers? They are merely together in a value delivery model to the end customer."

"Right, that makes sense and will also make Bill from Business Banking upset. However, let's park that for now. Then we have things we do for people where they have little to no choice. Our internal stakeholders."

"Which is why I find it funny when we have Product Owners, who are meant to represent the customer and prioritise the delivery to maximise the customer value and they are working on internal applications" Julie laughed in her awkward and worried way

"Good point, the product they are owning for most of our internal systems are user based and merely one cog in the wheel of the value chain."

"I had a thought today about this, my entire 30 strong team has zero links to the customer, we have project managers who are bringing us new work, we have maintenance we have to complete and lastly we serve internal stakeholders needs.

So if there are no customer interactions, we would likely see lower employee satisfaction and lower customer value delivered." Julie looked visibly upset by this reflection.

"It's ok Julie! First step in any change is to admit where you are now. Now we know a great pilot to trial more customer involvement?" Mark grinned, it didn't exactly make Julie feel better.

NZFS knew best

Julie's phone started ringing and before Julie answered Mark's phone started ringing at the same time. The minor pause said it all, Julie and Mark took their respective phone calls to realise its a P1 and the worst kind. It was a P1 with media attention. All technology leaders have been told they must come to level 28 immediately, which can't mean good news.

Mark and Julie arrived at Level 28, Greg was standing impassionately waiting for everyone to arrive and sit down. Mark and Julie took a seat with the other leaders, there were others in the auditorium, not just technology. Patrick the head of enterprise programme management was here, Alex the Chief Security and Information officer, Henry the Chief Marketing Officer and his team all sitting, looking like deers in lights. Julie thought to herself, this can not be good.

"On Thursday, we released three years of hard work. I thank you all for your commitment, yes, it took a year longer than expected, but it was released with only minor bugs. The executive team signed off on all complications and I want to reiterate that we are very pleased with the outcome. " Greg's openly was less than admirable, not only has he opened with a disclaimer but he also said all his peers are just to blame as himself. This isn't good.

"The release management did an exceptional job and we rolled out to all our users over the weekend with zero performance issues. I would like to say thanks to my team for putting in the hours to deliver such a robust new system. Over the weekend the users got to experience this new modular system and haven't quite understood our vision. Over social media we have seen thousands of complaints for missing features from the previous system and without consulting us, the mainstream media has published this as the worst upgrade in financial history. If they had spoken to us, we could have explained how to use the new system, this is a case of the problem with the customer not understanding the latest technology"

"Is he joking?" snapped Julie

Greg paused, looked in Julie's direction, that's when Julie realised she said that a bit too loud. Well you spoke up Julie, can't back down now.

"Excuse me Greg, this sounds like a fantastic release and well done to the delivery team, have we gone back to the customer testers and filtered the responses through them? I.e are these issues limited to a segmentation or was our sample size too small?"

Julie thought about her last company, they used to test in small batches and due to the sample size being too small, the results didn't match the release.

"Julie, your team tested this system, this is something you should know"

Julie raced her mind trying to think about this, yes she had a testing and quality assurance team, but this programme of work was being run out of the PMO, then it dawned on her, Stan, one of the project managers was filtering testing work through her team for PMO. However, her team didn't own testing, they were merely testing the functionality and performance.

"Yes, functional testing. However, my team is not the customer. They only test based on performance issues and if the requirements have been met. Who did the customer testing, how many people did we use, for how long and did we implement any variations?"

Patrick stood up playing with his glasses on route; "We had no requirements for customer involvement. We delivered exactly the requirements in the brief and it was rolled out to users from Thursday night. A successful three year programme. If someone wanted to test this with actual customers first, it would have delayed the release, something that was told to us is absolutely unacceptable."

"Just so we are clear; we didn't test with the customer, at what point did the customer give the requirements? As in when was the last confirmation that the features were in line with what they wanted?"

"Julie, you have COMPLETELY disrupted this session" Greg has lost his calm and steady look and resembles a snarling dog now. "We are here to raise how best to handle the media attention, how we can educate our customers on the benefits they have just received. This is why Marketing is here. Technology is here in case we have to double down and release more features and security is here to ensure that we don't rush and deliver something that breaks any regulations with how fast we will deliver a solution."

"I would say Greg" Henry was now standing near Greg, although Henry was younger than Greg, he seemed to calm him down with just a look and a few words. Must be the pony tail, thought Julie. "Julie is right. This media attention is not good, the reputation of NZFS is now at risk and this could snowball out of hand. The tech looks great, but we know we never talked to customers three years ago, let alone before going live. We implemented this solution based on requirements from the executive board. I remember I joined this role two years ago and asked the same question. Don't you remember? The solution was designed by the last CIO as a game changer, the documents are over five years old now. We have given the customers solutions we THOUGHT they wanted five years ago. So, I would recommend focussing on what they are saying, not on education. They are our customers, they know best, not us."

Measuring customer reactions

"Actually, that's a great idea Henry, Julie get your team to evaluate the complaints, create a prioritised list of changes and give to Patrick by close of business today; we will spin this from 'worst disaster' to 'NZFS listens to customers'. Yes, any marketing is good ,marketing, well done Henry." Greg finished by almost insulting everyone trying to help.

Henry looked at Julie, a look that said one thing, 'I will help don't worry'. Mark and Julie left, rang Simon the technical lead, Susan the business analyst and Jude the customer owner. They all met in the war room once more. However, this time, Paul from retail banking, Janet from Marketing, Jude from customer personas and Natalie from data and insights came in moments later.

"We are here!" Paul came in singing with a high pitched voice.

"Well, hello, can I help" replied Julie, who was trying not to be irritated by Paul's entrance.

"Well Julie, you can't start a movement where everyone helps and then expect us not to help when you need it. Our managers identified that this P1 requires us three from the value chain map and we heard how much fun the last session was. I am excited." Paul smiled and danced around the table.

Mark laughed, he knew Paul as they played tennis together, but that wasn't what made him laugh, he was laughing at Julie's face, no matter how 'fun' Julie thought she was, she knew deep down, fun was not her middle name. Serious may be a better description of how Julie was 90% of the time; this P1 needed serious discussion, however, it made sense to have more cognitive diversity so Julie smiled

"Thank you everyone for coming. You have the brief I assume?"

Everyone nodded, so Julie continued, "we have the go ahead for something quite remarkable at NZFS; we are going to focus solely on the customer. Remember as per Strategyzer: 72% of releases fail to receive positive uptake. Speaking of strategyzer, let's use their value proposition canvas."

Julie drew on the whiteboard a large circle..

"Inside the circle is the customer. We are lucky because this only impacted retail customers, however, let's not get lazy, we may find multiple niche customer segmentations when we get going, which will mean trying to serve all will lead to serving none. On the right hand side of the circle, we have the lists of all the jobs this customer wants to get done, this can be functional, social or emotional. The bottom of the circle we will highlight the pains in which the customer has, trying to achieve their chosen job. Finally up on the top of the circle will be customer gains, these are the ways our customers measure success, if they were to be successful in their job, it would be the benefits."

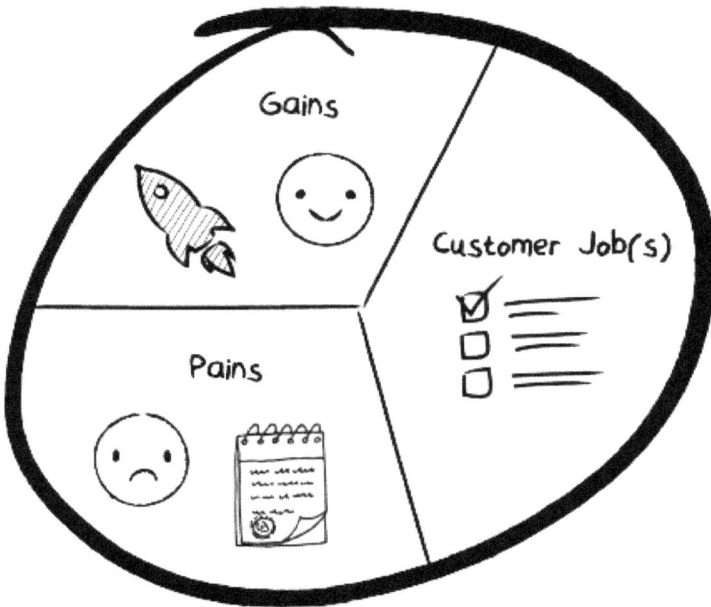

Adapted from Value Proposition Canvas | Strategyzer

Julie then drew a large square on the left hand side of the circle.

"We will list on the left hand side of the square the features our system now has, the bottom of the square will be the pains that the system completes for the customer, not what we believe, it has to match what they care about on the right hand side and on top will be gains that the system gives that match the customers desires. Put simply, we need to figure out what is the difference or delta between what the customer is expecting to get done, what pains they have, gains they want and what we just delivered. This difference will be the backlog for moving forward. "

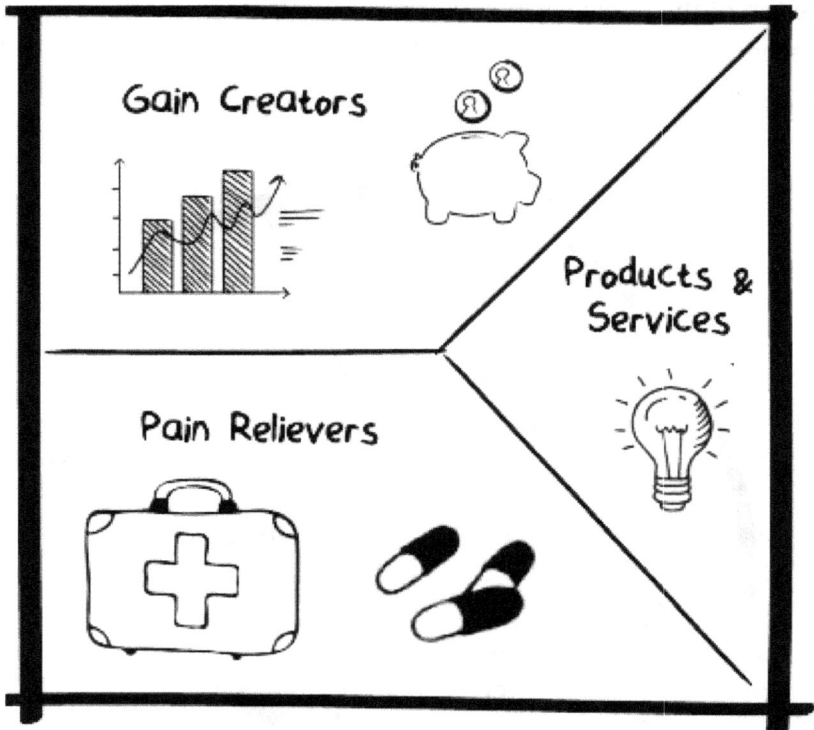

Adapted from Value Proposition Canvas | Strategyzer

"I want to collect all the complaints, compliments that have already been made, I want to ring 100 random customers that have logged in and NOT said anything and then we are going to create a prioritised list of changes. Are you ready? Who wants to do what?"

Paul jumped up with excitement, "I would like to ring 100 customers and gather feedback, I enjoy talking to retail customers."

"We need a marketing strategy for communication and a customer-centric roll out plan devised based on the feedback" said

Janet.

"I would like to run some scripts to gather the net promoter score over social media, emails, phone calls and gather all that data, segment it by gender, age and profession and then filter down to put on the value canvas" said Natalie, who looked like she wasn't expecting to be told yes.

"I would like to go over all the features from the documentation that was delivered and cross reference if any benefit realisation plan was put in plan and then try and understand if this links to what everyone else is doing" Simon was already working on this while he said it as he knew there was a lot to go through.

"Mark, should I bring down the 5 personas from the retail section?" Jude asked.

"Do you think it'll help" said Mark

"I do, if only to validate that there are five separate retail personas"

"You're the expert, let's do it" Mark took a sip of his water as Janet left the room happy.

Julie agreed "Mark is right, you are the experts, so I agree with all your plans and I believe we have the right cognitive diversity in the room to achieve our goals together. We have five hours remaining, it's going to be fun."

It was a tough five hours, Julie bought lunch for everyone and was ringing customers herself to help Paul. Mark was taking direction from Jude on how to adjust the five confirmed niche customer segmentations. Which by the end of the day really helped to understand what had happened.

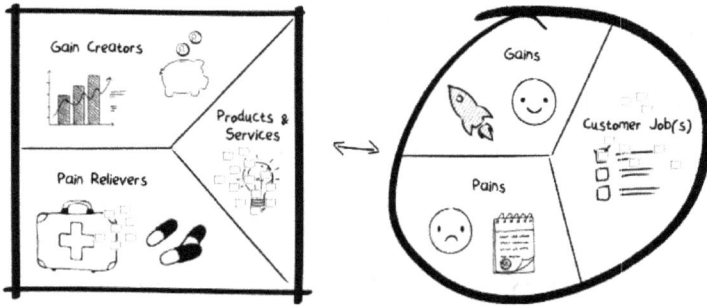

One of the customer segmentations was where 80% of the complaints were coming from. Males in major cities, within the first home buyer age group. A key strategic direction for NZFS and very worrying.

What they wanted to achieve from a day to day life with NZFS was just five simple jobs and since NZFS had rolled out the new system, they haven't been able to complete one very important job. They could not pay using their phone, watch or other device with near field communication.

With the feature list as long as the Sky Tower in Auckland and practically a five year programme of work, why was there no link to any popular automatic pay functionality. The confusing thing for Julie was that we never had this functionality, so they didn't lose anything?

"This makes sense now" Said Janet

Julie was confused but kept quiet

Natalie nodded, "it seemed like a mass revolt and those on

the phone were more upset then angry. They were complaining because they are upset, upset at the thought of moving providers."

"Sorry, I don't understand, NZFS never had this functionality, so why is it the main complaint?" Julie was very confused

"Expectations vs reality. These pains and gains are what really matter to the customer for NZFS, as you can see, we have a LOT of features we delivered but it only really mapped to two main pain points. The customer didn't need education, because the worst pains, we had missed."

Julie still looked blank at Janet. With her long history in marketing consulting and design thinking, she was obviously very used to this.

"We may be a financial services company with home loans, savings, investments and credit cards. That's how we delivered this new retail system, we delivered it as a bank doing products for people to buy. Let's call this customer Brad. Brad doesn't see NZFS that way, he see's NZFS enabling his ability to buy a flat white while out on a run, he feels that NZFS should be removing obstacles for a fluid experience in buying a house and he hears about all the amazing overseas financial services companies doing this. So when we did a massive hype of completely revamping our systems over three years... He was expecting something amazing. What he got, was a lot of widgets."

"Not all complaints were due to near field communication payments" said Simon

"No, but we have spoken to 100 people, scrubbed the data on 800 people and that seems to be the triggering point. Once they started there, it became a boulder running down the hill to another financial company to complain about everything that is wrong." said Natalie.

"So are you saying if we just implement the out of the box functionality from the two or three big pay providers on the system and then allow the customer to link their cards, it might stop the escalation and customers leaving?" Simon said half laughing. "I agree let's put it as number one but we have a lot to put on the priority list. I am literally "Brad" and NFC wouldn't make me bank with NZFS

There was a sudden silence. A realisation that a "Brad" was in the room and a now very embarrassed Simon had admitted he isn't a NZFS customer.

Julie and the others prioritised the other changes in priority of number of people impacted and cost to change, with the number one being the near field communication strategy.

"I want to go to Henry first, he is expecting us, " said Janet as she led the way towards the elevator. Julie, Simon and Mark followed, allowing the others to get some much needed rest.

Julie felt this might be a trap, she should be going to Gregs office, he was waiting and was calling since 4pm for his list to take to the board.

"How did everything go today?" said Henry as he leaned back on his faux leather recliner, put his feet up on his antique desk and ushered everyone to sit.

Janet explained the day, it was refreshing to see that Henry had no doubt they would complete and provide him with a plan. Unlike Greg who rang every 20 mins for an update.

"Simon, is this feasible to get done in the next two weeks? If I removed any roadblock we have internally?" Henry felt sure of himself that he could.

After Simon nodded and looked at Julie for reassurance, Julie was about to say something when

"Do it. It's a go"

Julie, Simon and Mark had no idea what was going on.

"It's done. " Said Janet.

"Wait, what has happened?" Just as Julie said that everyones phone went off. Janet had sent a company wide communication on all channels explaining that:

'After listening to our customers we are implementing a change in direction for our retail system, with the customer choosing the direction. Our first release next month will have Near Field Communication to allow walletless payment across all devices'

"Greg isn't going to like this, we can't just tell the internal people we are going to do something." Julie felt like she was behind.

"Not just internal. I have been writing a selection of media articles all day, I set up my Microsoft Automation, we now have social media, news articles, blog posts and we will follow up with videos tomorrow." said Jude.

"Let me talk with Greg Julie."

Julie looked at her phone, Greg is phoning. She left it and decided 6pm is late enough to answer work calls.

Greg kept phoning until 6:43pm. Then silence.

The next morning Julie started checking all the social media and online news.

It was strangely... positive. Everyone was talking about how great it is that NZFS got rid of their system and upgraded the moment their customers asked. Julie didn't reply that the system is not actually changing or that we are just adding new features and those features couldn't be added as fast without the system that everyone hated...

As she got into the office, Greg was waiting.

"I tried calling you last night" Greg said sternly

"I was so tired and I needed to get some sleep, have you seen the list of changes? Completed as you asked." Julie was trying to stay neutral

"Yes, very happy. Our CEO Rhonda said it was the best way forward, she is very happy with me leading the new customer and data analytics transformation on the back of the last CIOs terrible programme. Oh, Natalie has asked to join your team through her manager, I said yes as I need to get this transformation complete. You are welcome." Greg smiled and walked away.

Customer Experience Measures

Thankfully the rest of the week was calm and collected, Mark and Julie were able to slowly build up the customer-centric measurements because suddenly it was their job to transform. Yet they were not sure if Greg knew what the transformation would mean?

Customer at the Centre

Putting the customer at the centre of decision making ensures that the organisation is moving WITH the customer, not away from them.

Magenta: Our products are more important than our customers

Red: When revenues decline we blame the staff or customers

Amber: Personas are created by Design teams outside our Value chain or business unit

Orange: We understand who our customer is and what they need - persona, empathy maps and customer journey

Green: Customer has been brought into the team to develop and report back on changes instantly

---

Customer Feedback

Organisations that focus on the feedback from the customer are more likely to deliver superior products.

Magenta: Customer feedback is not required

Red: Uses Executive team as the customer

Amber: Feedback is requested after delivery of value

Orange: We have customer representative who gets regular and ongoing feedback direct from the customers

Green: Customer is part of the team, allowing us to make rapid decisions based on new feedback

Customer Alignment

Understanding your customer and aligning with their pains and gains, increases customer satisfaction.

Magenta: No alignment

Red: Each year your organisations strategy re aligns to the executive team

Amber: Each manager has a different view of customer value

Orange: Centralised vision for customer value but implemented by individuals differently

Green: All customer touch-points are aligned to a customer vision for great customer value that is agreed to with a customer

---

"This looks right Julie, so let's judge ourselves? Firstly my team do centralised personas and also do the direct marketing as I just found out from Janet. As for our customers at the centre, I think amber. I was leaning towards red with Greg blaming our customers and wanting to 'educate them', however, that's not what we do as an organisation, it's just Greg."

"Agreed" Julie paused and read the next one "Customer Feedback, well, we get feedback from customers, after delivery? "

"Yes, five years ago, we would have been Red. The entire point of that programme was because we used to use the executive teams as our customers, at least now we do seek out customer feedback." Mark was starting to realise the organisation had moved on since he joined.

"Customer alignment, we don't align with the executive team. I believe each business unit is trying to deliver customer value, but, we don't all agree how to measure customer value and which customer segmentation and why. So we are amber there as well."

Julie looked up at their almost complete business agility radar. Mark stood up to get a closer look, "this has been a great few weeks Julie. Not only are we almost there with a complete picture of our agility current state, but we have used this already to guide us on how to solve our issues.

We have focused on strategy, diversity and the customer. So I assume the entire left hand side is to do with people. Customer value and employee value. With the right hand side more focused on why and how we get the value complete."

Julie didn't realise she had drawn it that way, it reminds her of the harry potter film when they were reading tea leaves, but just so happened to be correct.

"That's exactly why I created it that way. Here is your homework, Empowering employees for greater business outcomes" Julie smiled and sat down, realising she may be able to leave at 4pm.

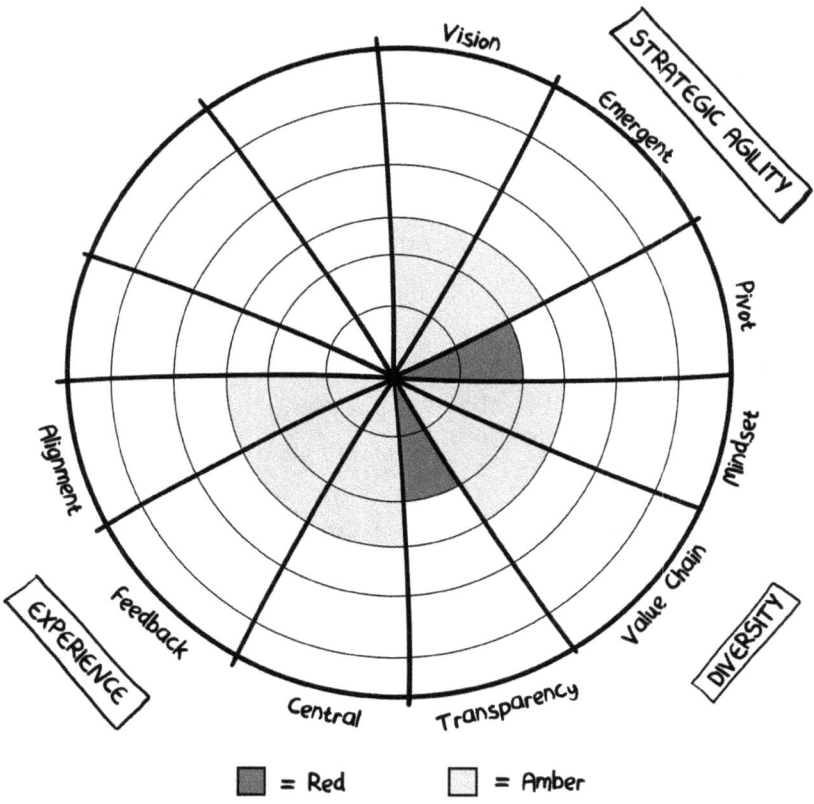

STRATEGIC AGILITY

Vision

Emergent

Pivot

Mindset

Value Chain

DIVERSITY

Transparency

Central

Feedback

EXPERIENCE

Alignment

■ = Red   □ = Amber

Employee Empowerment

Social Loafing

Groups can be fantastically unproductive due to their natural camouflage to hide individual effort. Under the cover of group-work, employees can do less productive work, happy in the knowledge that others are probably doing the same. And even if they're not: who'll know? This is what psychologists have called social loafing and it was beautifully demonstrated by a French professor Max Ringelmann as early as the 1890s.

Ringelmann, often credited as one of the founders of social psychology, instructed people to pull on ropes either separately or in groups of various sizes and he measured how hard they pulled. What he found changed what we thought about how groups worked. The more people that were in a group, the less effort they put in.

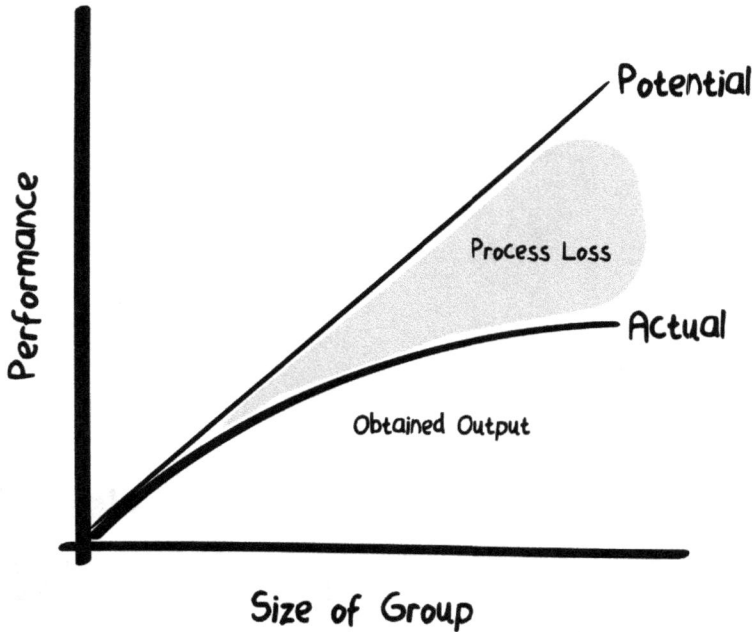

Since Ringelmann's original study, many others have found the same result using different types of tasks. Most entertainingly Professor Bibb Latané and colleagues had people cheering, shouting and clapping in groups as loud as they could. When people were in groups of six they only shouted at one-third of their full capacity.

The effect has been found in different cultures including Indians, Taiwanese, French, Polish and Americans, it's been found in tasks as diverse as pumping air, swimming, evaluating poems, navigating mazes and in restaurant tipping. However social loafing is less prevalent in collectivist cultures such as those in many Asian countries, indeed sometimes it is reversed.

It's not hard to see why this finding might worry people in charge of organisations. Noting that social loafing is most detrimental to the productivity of a group when it is carrying out 'additive tasks';

where the effort of each group member is summed. Not all tasks fit into this category. For example a group problem-solving session relies on the brains of the best people in the group – social loafing wouldn't necessarily reduce productivity in this group as markedly.

Humans are social creatures of habits. There are a few theories as to why we loaf. Firstly, it is said that it is a natural reaction to tribal evolution and it increases the less visible your specific tasks are in a group. When groups are larger, the individuals become more anonymous. Imagine you're doing something on your own: if it goes well you get all the glory, if it goes wrong you get all the blame. In a group, both blame and glory are spread, so there's less carrot and less stick, resulting in less proportional action.

Groups in organisations are formed from management with no clear social contract or purpose to seek higher goals; as per Herzberg's research in the 1950s, this will also create dissatisfaction and therefore less motivation through hygiene factors. The less a group agrees to the outcomes and rules of the group, the less motivation the group has, resulting in members of the group assuming others will perform the required actions.

What if you are not a loafer and you work hard? Eventually, you will become resentful and 'revenge loaf' or seek different employment opportunities[30]. Which is probably why great workers who are demotivated, become loafing workers after three months.

Lastly, we see that personal motivation and accomplishment is linked to individual loafing. If the task doesn't relate to the individual's personal goals, they are not motivated to perform the action in the team[31], this is especially true if there is no feedback from the team and if there is ambiguity in the task at hand[32].

Imagine if the team members are given tasks that have no

traceability back to higher customer goals, there is no way for the team members to feel a sense of accomplishment and they are in an environment where the teams have been forced together for the benefit of management, size ranging from 10 to 20. This is common practice for capital intensive projects with multiple teams, resulting in a potential loss of productivity up to 80%[33].

Employee Productivity Impact

A case study from New Zealand shows how managers can impact the motivations and productivity through creating teams without clear links to value, implementing Agile processes without the empowerment that comes from the Agile principles and shows us the importance of employee empowerment to best serve the needs of the customer.

[Company A] is a government agency that has an information and communications technology department (ICT). The ICT department has a multi-level hierarchy in which numerous individuals with a range of skills are hired to develop applications for frontline workers. People management is under four mid-management individuals, specialising in their discipline (project management, testing, development and business analysis), who report to the Head of ICT.

The individuals are part of two mixed discipline teams, split by project and are located sitting by their respective disciplines. It has been found that the process and framework was the result of a previous program retrospective, which is a form of group reflection on changes they wish to make as a team. However, upon evaluation of the documentation, it was found that the results were the decisions of the mid-management individuals and not the teams.

The team members lacked accountability, depending on task allocation from delegated leaders, forming an autocratic leadership, while maintaining a pseudo-Laissez-Faire environment. Task allocation to members has created a mentality of groupthink, based on self-interest, self-censorship and creating an illusion of unanimity[34]; this increases the risk of social loafing and reduces performance[35].

Team members likely have been disempowered by management in the process of creating the initial team; upon inspection, management created teams based on Taylorism methods, by selecting agents based on specialist skills for the up and coming project, instead of empowering the team members to self-organise and collaborate.

Although autocratic leadership can work in the short term, a team in the forming stage, yet made up of experts, will have better performance when they concern themselves with delivering value rather than looking for guidance. Teams that are not allowed to develop, suffer from reduced performance, role ambiguity and are restricted from continuous improvement.

Further, teams unable to self-organise; management has created dominant thought oriented teams, with monitor and specialist skill sets with the presumption based on Taylorism style of management for increased output. This validates the role of the Manager by performing an action and people-oriented role, ensuring idol-like characteristics from the team and creates further opportunity for control over the team[36].

It can be observed that teams at [Company A] lack cohesion, this may be due to the forming teams still seeking outside leadership. However, it is observable that team members have a sense of ambiguity as to which team they are a part of due to informal groups appearing among their disciplines. These conflicting dependencies can be compounded as their extrinsic rewards, comes from their discipline management, team members sit cohabitated within their disciplines, and learning and motivation is provided at a discipline level[37].

It has been shown teams can create unity through communication, leading to better productivity through collocation. Locating discipline teams together may be positive for management, creating a sense of inclusion within the discipline but has adverse effects on the performance output of the team[38]. Frequent face to face interactions allow customers and teams to avoid issues and complacency early on[39]

Some team members have shown minimal interest in the outputs of the delivery team in favour of their speciality tasks, disregarding calls to perform like a cross-functional team from other members of the delivery team, which has shown to reduce challenges[40]. Extrinsic motivation is used by management by associating KPIs with specialist outputs, rather than focusing on delivery team value, this increases alienation from the product and is further heightened by management controlling the labour process, resulting in fragmentation and performance issues[41]

Lack of autonomy of decision making leads to the questionable nature of if the delivery team is a team at all, or merely a workgroup pushing for individual needs[42].

Teams have a wide variation in motivation for the task, however, on average seem to be directional instead of meaning-making, awaiting tasks to be assigned to them and not actively involved in the customer output, shown to be an update best practice[43] and to enable teams for best performance[44]. Management saw no benefit in linking tasks to higher meanings to showcase the benefits of each task, instead of relying on Taylorism style management to merely pay more external contractors to complete the piece of work given to them.

This process becomes hit and miss due to the wide variety of needs of team members that may or may not fit into the goals of [Company A] as per Levinson's ego driven motivational theory. Without a link between the benefit to the customer, feedback from the customer and the specific task a team member is completing; there is less motivation[45] in completing or organising tasks for visibility. Lack of visibility and motivation are critical drivers of social loafing and reduced performance[46].

Reflection practices are not taken seriously, with team members not wanting to complete the meetings and that they are a "Waste of time". The teams were led to believe they would have a say in the process and will use reflection to improve continuously. Reflection on the process allows better performance, improved teamwork, higher motivation and mitigating errors[47]. This is understandable as Scrum Masters were brought in to force Scrum on the team without their consent.

[Company A] teams were found to have reflection meetings. However, the management teams used the outputs of reflections to make decisions on behalf of the teams with the reasoning that they owned the process and the time outputs were more of a concern to them.

Strengths of this process include short-term delivery performance based on the presumption of external contractors; however, in this case, the performance would decline over time due to known coercion and cause [Company A] increased expenses in higher turnover of team members[48]. Over a three month period, [Company A] had a higher turnover of staff, a 60% reduction in productivity across the unit and had to increase spend by 144% on external contractors to achieve the deadlines.

This Taylor version of management does not allow feedback from the experts to help reshape future outputs and creates an authority-compliance management balance by disregarding concern for people; this clear manipulation causes low performance..

Upon identifying management decisions that dictate team structure, team locations, disregarding lessons learnt and autocratic leadership over their discipline. Management has a benefit to protect their positions[49] and leverage micro-politics to exploit transformation behaviours; this allows them to manage a team instead of employing super leadership techniques that results in happier employers and increased business outcomes[50], however, this reduces the need for the managers who feel threatened.

Understanding this point of view, the evidence shows why motivation is reduced, how teams will fail to adapt and grow , how performance is reduced (and how employee satisfaction would be low)[51]

This second part of the case study will provide steps that based on scholarly evidence will mitigate the problems, a detailed analysis as to why this will help and how it can be implemented with least disruption to current working practice for other leaders in the future.

Although autocratic leadership can be said to help drive a solution away from selfish behaviour's[52], this is not a need for the [Company A], as team members are already looking to achieve what is required, it is, however, the ambiguity in what they are meant to deliver, that is the concern.

Problems with the lack of accountability can be driven from not being empowered to make decisions, teams that take on more responsibility, will step up and be accountable for their tasks as long as the team believes management is authentic. Transforming teams for empowerment will mean enabling their decisions; this means allowing teams to look at how they deliver work and self-organise into the team best suited to complete that work.

Teams that are highly motivated and are the experts in their tasks may work in a Laissez-Faire environment productively,[53] however, at the forming stage of the team, it is best to ensure management are leading the teams to independence, instead of being hands off. Therefore, team democracy, with management in the democratic decision-making seat, may be the best initial step in transferring the forming teams with no accountability into self-organising accountable teams. [54]

To remove any form of ambiguity, a social contract between management and teams would allow them to feel secure, a supported work climate can help teams feel autonomous and thus satisfy their ability for empowerment[55].

Cohesion within a team allows for connections among the team. Teams that work together in collaboration with their customers have the highest chance for performance. Teams collocated together have better communication and collaboration, regular communication ensures better team cohesion[56].

After enabling teams to self-organise, it can be part of the next phase to see if they wish to be collocated together as well, surrounded by their specific and valuable work. To strengthen further team cohesion, management can focus on a sense of unity, outside group activities or charity events, to take team members outside of the work environment and build social cohesion.

Each team should feel as if their work has meaning and is of value, the value they perform on a task should have traceability back to a broader customer goal, with customer feedback; this leads to increased motivation internally rather than from management[57]. The correct work suited to the self-organising teams can be negotiated with the team about a preferred delivery time based on other work priorities from the customer.

When teams are self-organised and are located comfortably, the customer-focused task can be allocated to the teams with links back to how they are fixing a specific benefit of the customer. Teams who can visualise the benefit to the customer will increase in team motivation, and it will also help build intrinsic motivation through team cohesion as the team can see the impact of their work.

Care must be monitored through continuous improvement to seek how much autonomy [Company A] professionals should have, as reduced performance may be seen if team members do not cross-collaborate and stay as specialists[58].

By enabling the teams to be autonomous for a period, reflection should become more "believable" to the teams. Empowering the teams as Superleaders, management can focus on the teams continuously improving their processes for best performance and well-being[59]. Recommendation after each piece of value produced and SuperLeaders should ensure that at this time, collaboration with other teams allows for cross-pollination of ideas for improving team motivation and performance, without the need for managers[60].

Concerns for teams not wanting to participate in learning a variety of skills should dissipate after ownership of the process is moved to the team[61]. However, the team should be continuously motivated to seek out new ways of doing the tasks assigned to them as a diversity of viewpoints allows for a successful output and if management actively propose the idea of cross-functional training, this may mitigate any hierarchical push back and promote benefits like scope creak mitigation.

Further cross-functional teamwork will allow the team to focus on delivering value, thus moving the team through to a performing team with mastery and autonomy, from forming and relying on management[62]

As part of this individual case study, four key problems within the [Company A] behaviour were identified: lack of accountability, team cohesion, no interest in cross collaboration and lack of motivation. These four problems have been analysed and have been linked back to potential causes delivered from mid-management with the fictitious understanding that this would create higher productivity, something that scholarly data has confirmed is not true.

This case study has shown how these problems can cause long-term future problems for [Company A] and most other companies with a higher turnover of staff and low performance. However, this analysis has shown from objective evidence that these problems can be mitigated with the enablement of the team to think for itself, locating the teams in delivery benefit, not specialist silos, create end to end value traceability with views of how the customer benefits and promote cross-functional training to promote how much value each individual team member can give.

From this case study and scholarly data, empowerment, autonomy, motivation and team culture are key areas of concern for any manager looking for performance results. Not only do these allow for higher productivity but we can now see how they will help mitigate social loafing which can be detrimental to any project or product upgrade.

Studies around motivational theory from the likes of Hogan and Vroom show us that intrinsically linked motivation is linked to lower social loafing, with a key push towards task variability.

When employees think the task is important, they do less loafing. Zacarro (1984) found that groups constructing 'moon tents' worked harder of they thought the relevance of the task as high, thought they were in competition with another group and were encourages to think the task was attractive.

So if the tasks are variable, important and in line with the team members idea of purpose. The motivation for the work will outweigh any reason for social loafing.

When the group is important to its members they work harder. Worchel et al. (1998) had people building paper streams in two groups, one which had name tags, matching coats and a sense of competition. Compared to a group given none of these, they produced 5 more paper streams.

Decreasing the 'sucker effect'. The sucker effect is that feeling of being duped when you think that other people in the group are slacking off. Reducing or eliminating this perception is another key to a productive group.

Teams that start to dehumanise, can separate themselves from the group and thus not empathise with the group. To fix this, the groups must work as a team, building outside of work relationships to see themselves as equal in purpose[63]. Social identity theory tells us that similarities build trust and those relationships mean less loafing.

Team Culture is huge in all aspects of business, with social loafing as a major risk, teams need to spend more time together in activities that are not work, they need to identify with the group, share a common purpose and spend longer than eight weeks as a team, to allow those relationships to grow.

Lastly, leaders who are respected are more likely to have higher performance per staff member[64]. Having teams self organise, control their process, create a social contract and enable them to deliver outputs in a way that suits them as a unit, means this unit will focus on delivery rather then Facebook[65].

If human nature is to loaf when things are a little in the dark. Agile Delivery can be a solution; by putting everything visible voluntarily, the more visible the better, tasks should be seen by any person in the organisation (preferably randomly), the tasks should be able to be understood by a layman and they should be traceable not only to larger pieces of work but to the benefit the customer is receiving!

This highly motivated part of Agile is designed to make us accountable for our tasks, which not only shows (as per motivational theory) to be productive but also allows mitigation of natural aspects of social loafing. To push this fact home, the motivational theory also tells us that feedback from the customer is also more important than our manager, so having the end user give feedback will stop what Karl Marx would call, alienation.

Allowing teams to self-create is rare, however, this type of Superleadership, allows teams to see the problem and self-assemble; which will also see them going through the team stages to perform a lot faster (assuming you do not break the team and reassemble for another project).

Once teams are together and empowered to design the correct process to match the work, set up a social contract on how they like to work, they will naturally want to sit together and socialise and only some minor 'help' would be needed to make them feel trusted.

Back to work!

It was Saturday night, Julie was sitting down in her comfy slippers, a cup of milo and binge watching the New Zealand Block from last week, when Mark messaged on her Teams application. Julie tried to ignore it, but just in case it was important, she opened the application.

Mark: This paper was hard to read

Julie: Yes, my leadership professor really pushed my academic delivery

Mark: Took me an hour but I am REALLY happy I took the time to get through it properly.

Mark: Was it about NZFS?
Julie: No, the case study was another company. It's eerie how similar everyone is

Mark: Did you fix them?

Julie: Fix is a strong word, I merely guided them back to making decisions themselves, connected them with their customers and removed their Scrum Framework, allowing them to choose how work was done.

Mark: Fascinating. See you Monday.

Julie: Good night Mark.

~

Julie had finished getting the kids ready for school, she got her flat white from her regular barista and enjoyed the nice Auckland harbour stroll to the office. Going up the escalators, she was wondering; 'will Mark be at the top, be in the war room, or for once, did I make it here first?

Sitting down at her desk, it felt far too quiet, until she opened her email.

From Greg

Hi Julie,

As the prime minister has lowered the Covid restrictions, I want everyone back in the office. Any contractors that do not agree, will not be extended.

Kind Regards,

G

Permanent vs Contractors

"Is this Greg trying to sabotage the NFC project? Surely not" Julie thought to herself. Looking at the HR records, it looks like everyone's contracts were up for renewal in a month. At least there was no risk of that project failing, however, there were 40% of her staff on contracts with all of them having at least one work-from-home day a week.

Julie: Hey Greg, just to clarify, did you want everyone back in the office five days a week?

Greg: No. Permanent staff may have two days to work from home if they choose, but contractors must be in the office five days a week.

Julie: Ok, do you think that might cause some clashes between contractors and permies?

Greg: They are contractors, if they want the benefits, they should join us properly.

"Well that cleared that up, I now have to tell twelve people they need to work in the office five days a week while also asking them to extend their contracts. Fun." Julie pondered what sort of ramifications there may be, I mean she loves coming into the office, others surely would like it too?

Hi All,

Great news, the Prime Minister lowered the restrictions again last night to near zero. We are finally free and it's safe to return to work full time. NZFS would love to see you in the office full time from next week.

Also great news, due to the recent upgrades, contract extensions will be automatically extended for six months.

Kind Regards,

Julie

Not much time after Julie sent the email, Simon came up to Julie's desk with a worried look on his face.

"Hey Julie, about your email" said Simon

"It comes from up top, I can not change it Simon" Julie responded quickly.

"I get that, but now we have a problem. In the developer channel the contract devs have stated they won't be extending, but worse than that, two have given notice to their agencies already! Normally I wouldn't be too concerned but Bob and Chris have been here since Covid lockdown version 1.0, so they have been here for three years. If they leave in two weeks, I won't be able to get our end of the NFC upgrades complete. Let alone the fact they have a lot of intellectual property." Simon paused but then decided to stop.

"Wow. ok, that's not good. It seems all contracts have been set up with contractors filling the gap, but their contracts are only set up for the duration of the project" Julie sighed

"Why would we need the contractors past the project they were hired for?" Simon was confused and it showed Julie just how project focused her team was.

"The great contractors vs permanent debate is as old as I am. We must remember, we are all on the same team and there isn't much difference between us. They help the supply and demand curve when we need more people; and they take on risk of that workload ending. The problem is when contractors are still here many years later.

Anything over a year seems confusing, we should have more permanent staff. There will always be more projects, more product development and more technical debt to remove. We should be focusing on creating a good team and if the demand for more value increases, we then bring on contractors to smooth out the delivery.

We have twelve contractors and now we haven't set ourselves

up to bring in permanent people. The Market is booming and everyone is leaving jobs, left right and centre. We need to move to a continuous delivery system and not a project system."

Agile vs Agility

Simon looked shocked "Do you mean Agile? We are already Agile!"

"Simon, Agile delivery is such a small part of how an organisation functions. When I talk about continuous delivery, I mean the delivery system, but also the human resources, financial measurements of value being delivered per person and how we integrate into the rest of the company.

Right now, our thirty people are delivering in an agile delivery framework, but how the projects come to us, how the people are allocated and how we draw down funding is causing us pain. We need the ability to adapt across our product streams, which will allow the agile delivery to be most effective."

Julie got up and drew one of the value chains that her and Mark were working on with a picture of multiple people, each person representing a team.

"Here is your team following the values of agile, however, the wider organisation is still focussed on static planning, governance and their products. This is the difference between Agile Delivery and Organisational Agility.

Simon pondered the whiteboard and realised how small the agile delivery function is.

"So we need to make the rest of the organisation Agile? An Agile Transformation"

Julie chose her words carefully, she knew that within technology agile was almost a go to fix for anything that is perceived as 'wrong'.

"Not quite. Agile or adaptive iterative delivery is good for complex environments that have a low cost of change. This is why the

Agile Manifesto was written by technology leaders and their lightweight frameworks were all about delivering technology solutions.

Business Agility is how the organisation adapts to respond to the customers needs in a flexible way. It has a lot of similarities, but it is the whole organisation doing what is best for the organisation and their customers. Which could mean no Agile.

How adaptive, responsive and flexible your organisation is, will be aligned to your culture, competitive advantage, goals and customers. Where Agile delivery tends to focus on values and principles that you either do or don't do. Agility is a spectrum that you constantly measure and stop changing once your customer metrics do not increase relative to the cost."

Simon looked back at the white board and then back at Julie, "Well, that makes sense, we have banking licenses, infrastructure, retail products as well as technology. Each one of our value chains will be different and components inside the value chain may need different delivery systems?"

"That is absolutely correct" Julie gave a sigh of relief. Simon wasn't an evangelical.

"Although I enjoy these interesting chats, what do we do about the contractors..... I mean our team members?"
"If we agree that they are team members, that they are supplying the important job of our capacity issues, then we need to set up something more continuous. I tried that in the email about six month contract extensions, but I think we need to make it more obvious.

If I send out an email to the contractors specifically and if you could talk to them. We will fix our resource requirements and their contracts will be about outcomes and not our projects, ensuring they can work on more than just the project they were hired for."

Hi All

I would like to thank you for working with NZFS and wanted to let you know the changes I am making for how contracts are supplied in the future.

We are moving to continuous delivery, where we will prioritise every outcome given to us and deliver the highest priority item. This means we will all work as a team, rather than splitting by project.

Kindest Regards,

Julie

The next two days went by and all but one contractor stayed and showed good support for the continuous delivery model. Those that were upset about the project they were on, were relieved that the project being canned did not mean they would be given notice.

"We lost Bob" Julie said to Mark.

"You only lost one contractor?!" Mark looked shocked, "others have lost half a dozen or more, and the moving back to the office hasn't gone very well, it's like pent-up aggression has exploded with contractors and permanent staff now separating. Terrible team dynamics, thanks to upper management!"

"When I reread employee engagement paper, it reminded me

that my chosen leadership style is coaching, I really enjoy asking questions and allowing the team to grow through thinking of the question themselves. I found myself facilitating this week and the staff have responded well.

The business agility radar is showing us that the culture is amber. If thats what everyone is used to, which is management, efficient and instructional style of leadership. If I use coaching style of leadership, they look lost, confused and uncomfortable.

Yet if I focus on facilitation style of leadership, where I help them achieve outputs they decided with goals I have worked with them on. I am getting better results. "

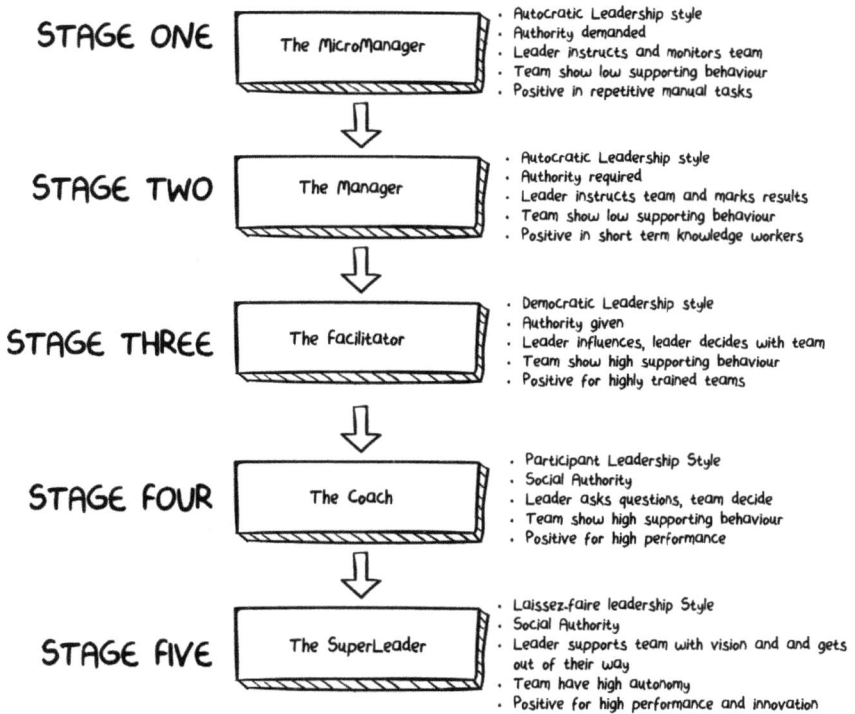

STAGE ONE — The MicroManager
- Autocratic Leadership style
- Authority demanded
- Leader instructs and monitors team
- Team show low supporting behaviour
- Positive in repetitive manual tasks

STAGE TWO — The Manager
- Autocratic Leadership style
- Authority required
- Leader instructs team and marks results
- Team show low supporting behaviour
- Positive in short term knowledge workers

STAGE THREE — The Facilitator
- Democratic Leadership style
- Authority given
- Leader influences, leader decides with team
- Team show high supporting behaviour
- Positive for highly trained teams

STAGE FOUR — The Coach
- Participant Leadership Style
- Social Authority
- Leader asks questions, team decide
- Team show high supporting behaviour
- Positive for high performance

STAGE FIVE — The SuperLeader
- Laissez-faire leadership Style
- Social Authority
- Leader supports team with vision and and gets out of their way
- Team have high autonomy
- Positive for high performance and innovation

Julie completed a hypothesized leadership matrix with agility culture.

"As a leader, if we want to help our people reach more empowered and innovative culture, we need to ensure we are only one level ahead at all times. To help our people, we need situational leadership.

Situational leadership is where your style of leadership changes based on the situation you are in. When we measure our agility, we need to be the leader where our people are, not where we want them to be.

As a salesman once told me, no one buys the tofu ice cream, the easier sell is a standard cone with added sprinkles. We need to just add the sprinkles, be slightly different, so that they feel comfortable with the change. "

Learning curve

"This makes sense" Mark stood up, "in change management we talk about change fatigue and staying within the learning curve of the team"

"What is the learning curve Mark"?

"Wait, is it time?" Julie looked impatient. Mark didn't notice and continued. "Is it finally time for Mark to show Julie something???"

"Very funny" Julie said

"Humans have a natural learning curve, we all love to learn and adapt, however, its all within reason. If its too much change too fast, our fear receptors kick in and we fight the change.

If the change is too slow then we get bored and become unproductive. The sweet spot is to continuous adapt the individual or team at a pace that is within the boundaries.

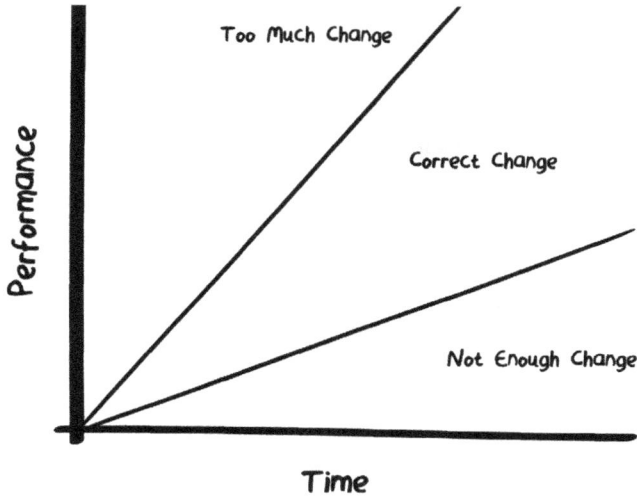

When we add this natural learning curve to the kubler ross curve, which are the stages humans go through when change is made. It is also called the five stages of grief! Humans tend to go through denial, anger, bargaining, depression, and finally acceptance.

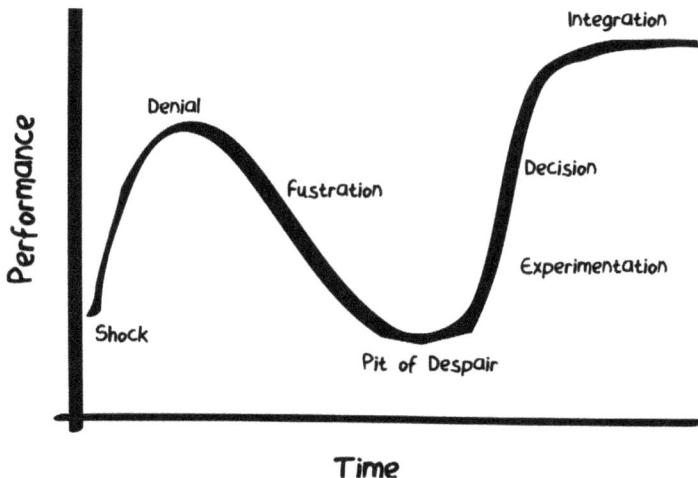

Adapted from Five stages of grief | Elisabeth Kübler-Ross

If the change is big, you run a much larger risk of causing pain to the employees, with denial or the pit of despair being outside their learning tolerance.

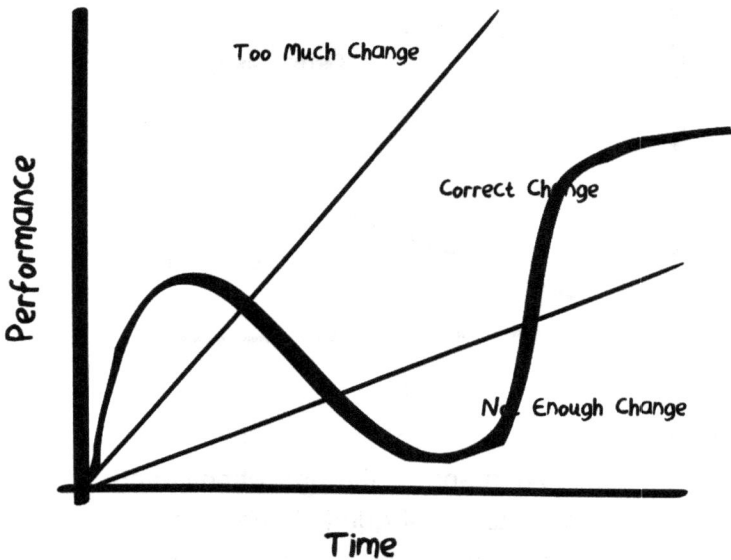

Whereas, if you focus on smaller changes. Adding sprinkles to the ice cream, then a flake, then reducing milk content. Maybe they will eventually like a tofu ice cream and be telling their friends?"

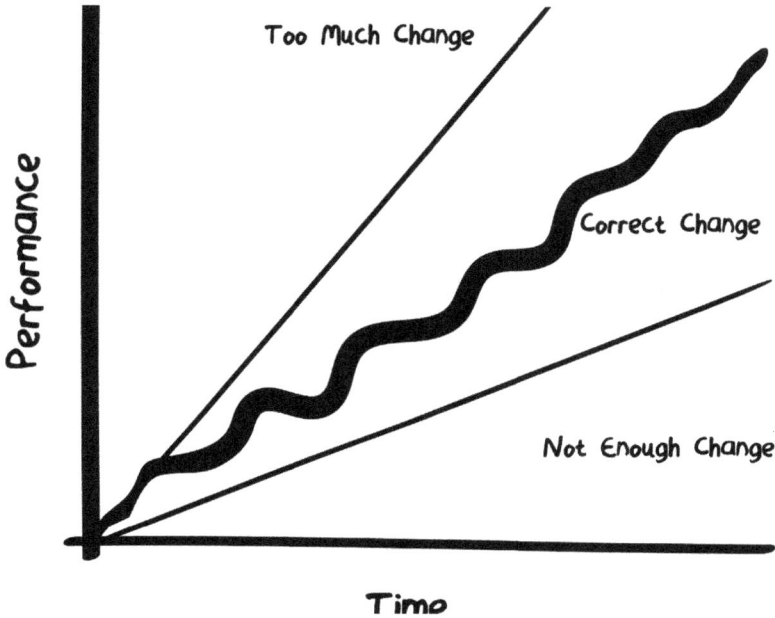

Too Much Change

Correct Change

Not Enough Change

Performance

Timo

"Nicely done, this logic sits well with what I was thinking as well. We are about to finish the Business Agility Radar, it'll give us our current state and we also know our vision for the future, which will give us a strategy and a form of measurements.

There is only one thing I am not convinced of."

"Whats that" Mark said

"No one ever really likes tofu ice cream" Julie attempted another joke.

Mark didn't smile. As a vegan, he must really like tofu ice cream.

Mark continued: "Lets finish the employee empowerment values?"

"Absolutely. We had some great lessons this week to back up

the case study as well. Leadership is key for empowered employ-ees, ensuring the structure of the people is set up for success"

"Agreed, then there is how the employees deliver work, I know you want this to be about agility but we should measure the agile delivery as it creates a better picture."

"That is fine, lastly, we should have continuous improvement, we are moving into continuous delivery and if we do not continu-ously improve, the teams will never own the outcomes themselves."

Mark and Julie worked on the wording of the questions and then scored themselves over the next two hours.

Employee Empowerment Measures

Agility for People

How leaders structure their people around value and how hiring impacts intrinsic motivation.

Magenta: We have mostly contractors

Red: Contractors are brought in for programmes of work and then released upon delivery

Amber: Teams have been created for project delivery (i.e. Scrum) with a focus on consistency

Orange: Autonomous teams have been created with individual KPIs and management lines and/or team members have titles with individual responsibilities

Green: Teams are self organising with authority over what work they complete and have access to the customer AND have group ownership of work with leaders who coach the team

---

Agile Delivery

The ability to deliver value and adapt moving parts in a complex environment drives greater motivation and empowers employees for success.

Magenta: No work is being started or complete

Red: Work is given to teams to do, not all work is complete before new work begins

Amber: Teams break work down into small tasks for use in a process governed by executives

Orange: Organisation have implemented an organisational framework that works across the value stream

Green: Teams create their own process based off of objective data of past events

---

Kaizen

Ensuring continuous improvement in an organisation creates innovation and the ability to pivot on the customer needs. However, it can't happen effectively without leadership empowerment.

Magenta: There is no continuous improvement process

Red: We transform our way to improvements through technology or restructures

Amber: There is a process improvement team looking for ways to increase efficiency

Orange: A leader measures outcomes to see if improvements can be made - such as Six Sigma

Green: We use data to continuously test new hypothesis and record the outcomes to make team decisions

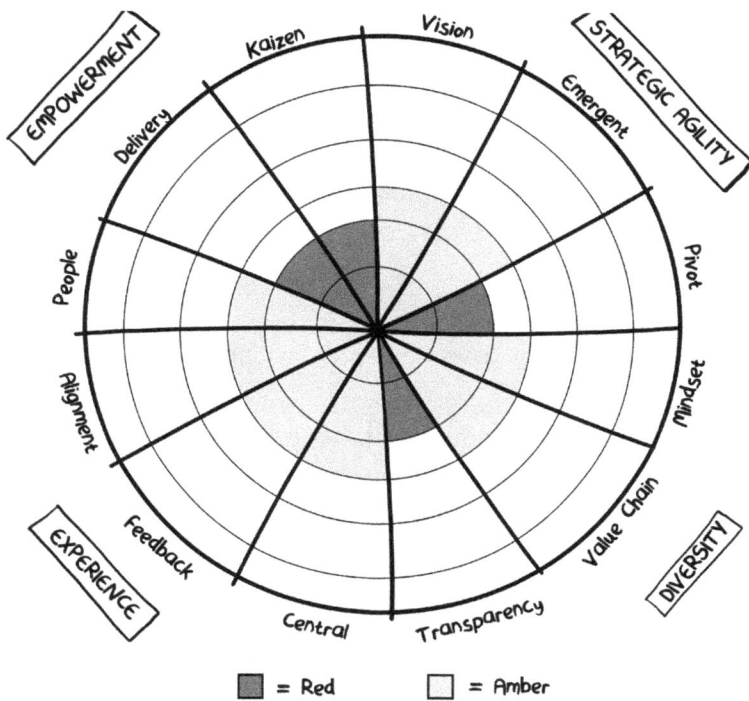

EMPOWERMENT — Kaizen, Vision — **STRATEGIC AGILITY** — Emergent — Delivery — People — Pivot — Alignment — Mindset — **EXPERIENCE** — Feedback — Value Chain — **DIVERSITY** — Central — Transparency

■ = Red   □ = Amber

"Oh dear. Two reds?" Mark said

"It makes sense when you think about it. My teams thought they were doing scrum but really it was project managers directly giving them work and you yourself said NZFS is constantly transforming in order to find new people. We don't invest in continuously improving our people."

"Well, at least we know our limitations. We do not empower our people to be the best they can be. We tell them what to do and expect success.

Now our current state is complete, we can see we have four red zones to work on. Should we start there?"

"I suspect you are right, however, how can we prove what we

Employee Empowerment   153

change has had an impact? Our KPIs are all lagging indicators, it'll be years before we can prove the changes we made had any impact.

We need some leading indicators. Things we can measure as soon as possible, that we can logically say will be linked to better business outcomes."

"Let me guess, my reading hasn't stopped?"

Julie hands Mark a paper on how to measure Customer Value. Mark laughed and it is with this moment he realised, Julie has had everything planned out from the start, he is HER champion, not the other way around.

"Hey, at least its Wednesday and not Friday?" Julie said with a smile.

Customer Value

What is Customer Value

Organisational design is made up of many attributes, including process, structure, technology and people[66]. Although leaders focus on strategic planning, research shows that it is the capabilities that produce a greater reward. The flexibility of a company and how often that company adapts to external information has a positive correlation with performance[67].

Organisations trying to obtain a competitive advantage in their industry need to be able to pivot quickly, adapt to new ways of working and be flexible in their approach, design and deliverables. Organisations need to focus on areas of their design to ensure the capabilities and behaviour can best deliver customer value. Leaders focus on strategic planning, however, the ability to rely on planning is diminishing[68].

In this literature review, I will define customer value and its links to financial performance, create a model for measuring customer value and then show the link between structure and customer involvement on customer value.

To understand how customer value impacts financial performance, we need a definition that can be widely accepted, measured and scaled. Metrics allow an objective lens on the impact on customer value from external capabilities.

Value is defined differently within various industries. Organisations can measure value by the value created. Porter positions that value is created only for the shareholders. When we discuss value from a Marketing perspective, it is customer-oriented and therefore value consumed.[69]

Customer value can also be described as the benefit the customer obtains from the company. The amount of value that a customer obtains could be inside the price that they are willing to pay, part of the brand loyalty a customer gives that company. Measured in the customer satisfaction or a combination of[70].

Stephan Liozu reviews the many variations of customer value, specifically the difference between value creation vs. value captured. Although the company may be creating value for the customer, the customer hasn't agreed to the value until they have consumed it. Measuring the value based on the products/services produced doesn't allow the Market to decide the true value. The value created by the organisation but not consumed by the customer is waste, although shareholder value can be customer value, it is an inferior metric due to the customer value may cause conflict between short term profit and long term sustainable customer value.

Sales are also a form of value consumed, however, sales do

not take into consideration the quality metrics from the customer, the sales alone will only determine the perceived value[71].

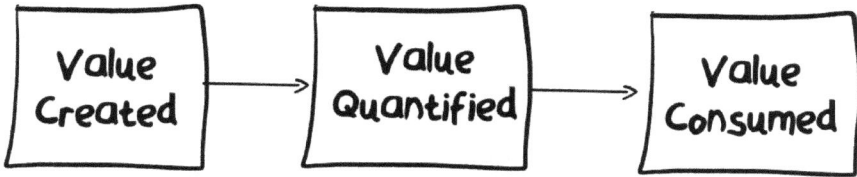

| Value Created | → | Value Quantified | → | Value Consumed |

Stephan Liozu states that customer value consumed is the difference between the value created and the quantification of that value. The higher the customer value consumed, the higher the potential financial performance through competitive advantage.

Value can be captured through price, once the value is fully understood, otherwise, the organisation could be mispricing and therefore reducing their competitive advantage.

Value quantification can happen during pricing through negotiation. However, the price can not be the only metric in customer value[72]. Using tools such as a customer journey map will allow further value quantification; a customer journey map will allow the organisation to empathise with the value being created, ensuring a real benefit is being recorded to the customer[73].

The ongoing loyalty from customers increases the number of sales per person and reduces onboarding cost of each subsequent sale, thus the brand loyalty can be a metric for customer value. The quality of the product or service can only be determined at the end of a sale, measuring customer satisfaction can give validation of the customer value consumed.

Liozu evidence is theoretical with no measures in place to allow leaders to see how they are quantifying their value. Research that shows metrics to be used to measure value quantification would ensure leaders can measure progress against actions they take.

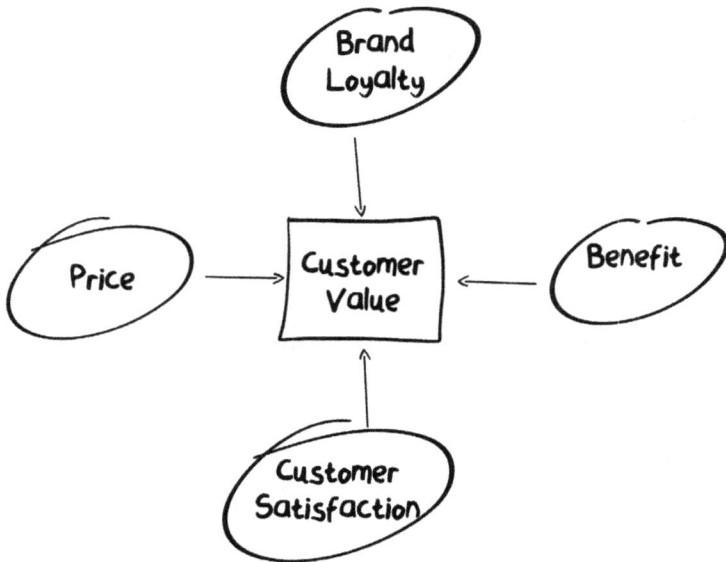

Customer value is the ability for organisations to add value to resources, measured by price that the customer is willing to pay, the loyalty of brand equity the customer is willing to give, the customers' satisfaction and the functional benefit the customer receives. These four inputs have been derived by the author while investigating the variations of customer value[74].

Measuring Customer Value

Knowing what to measure for customer value is only the first step, using the four inputs this study needs to understand how to measure them objectively to ensure they can be linked to financial performance.

The customer may receive social benefits, emotional benefits, functional benefits and have a perceived value, measured by customer satisfaction scores. Measuring customer satisfaction can be a good way to measure the value being consumed after the sale. In Yao et al study, moderate to strong correlations were found on the benefits a customer receives and negative correlations on costs and acquisition costs. Showing that customers found value in social, emotional and functional benefits.

The benefit to the customer can come in multiple ways; corporate social responsibility (CSR) has grown in popularity, this social benefit correlates with financial performance. Ali et al found that by focusing on social benefits, organisations can increase the brand value at a lowered cost, driving greater financial performance[75].

Hedonic Value, which is the value of the experience of the customer, is made up of the end to end experience with the product, the company and the purchase. Hedonic value had a greater correlation with return on assets (0.07), earnings per share (0.11) and loyalty (0.35) than overall value, satisfaction and utilitarian value.

Satisfaction is the measure at the end of the purchase, the overall value is the net benefit to the customer after purchase and utilitarian value is the ability to complete a transaction efficiently.

Customer satisfaction is positively correlated to financial performance yet this is the historical value of the customer captured in data. Golovkova et al. found the customer satisfaction index measured as earnings per share (EPS) had a strong positive correlation with the financial performance of the banking industry, a highly competitive industry (2019). Sun and Kim found moderate positive correlations on financial performance including return on assets and return on equity using customer satisfaction as a metric[76].

Brand equity is a Marketing standard. Brand equity is a concept that gives value to a customer's perception pre, during and post-purchase[77]. Verbeeten and Vijn measured business performance with brand equity; they determined that it created a point of difference, which created greater financial performance[78].

The ability to charge a larger margin on top of the resource price is linked to greater financial performance. Perceived value from the customer shows us that they are willing to pay more as they believe they are receiving greater value.

Those that focus on profit, do not outperform the organisations that focus on customer value. In Ziyambi's study of financial performance, they found a direct correlation between South African organisations that focused on customer value over focusing solely on profit[79].

Branding, customer satisfaction, price and benefit are linked to each other either directly or indirectly. Using the four inputs to define customer value, a leader can measure the hedonic value consumed by the customer, then by strategically deciding to change one or more of these inputs, customer value will increase or decrease. The literature shows a positive correlation with each of the inputs of increasing customer value and the financial performance of a company[80].

For every $1 invested in customer value in large organisations, $6 was the average return on investment across all customer value metrics. Hedonic value shows the in-flight customer value as well as the end result. Hedonic value is the end to end value, where brand and benefits show a weak positive correlation with earnings per share and return on assets. Organisations can use hedonic value as a description for the end to end customer value, however, this study has broken down customer value into four specific measurable assets.

This study has shown that increased financial performance can be obtained if organisations focus their strategy on greater customer value. Instead of focusing on the financial return, an organisation can focus on the customer and the four inputs that help that objective. Increased brand loyalty, customer satisfaction, functional benefit realisation and price can be measured via key performance indicators (KPIs) to ensure the organisation is heading in the right direction to achieve customer value.

To increase customer value via customer value inputs, organisations must rapidly challenge themselves to test new ways of working. To chase new ways of working that measure against customer value, an organisation must be designed to meet those needs. With the correct organisational structure to match the customer and the ability to get rapid direct feedback, this study believes that this will lead to achieving customer value, resulting in greater financial performance.

If an organisation's competitive advantage is decreasing in their industry, the organisation has enough funds to perform a transformation and the organisation has the right leadership to sustain the change iteratively, then this author believes that re-structuring around the customer will increase customer value and thus increase competitive advantage, resulting in greater financial performance.

To decrease risks and initial cash outlay, recommendations have been created to realise their potential. The organisation's strategic goal to increase customer value, although a great goal, it is not measurable. A continuous improvement plan behind a clear objective would allow a transformative leader to find bespoke ways to obtain the customer structure.

This study can recommend two metrics that associate with each, these KPIs indicate customer value is increasing and were used by the successful sample case studies. It would be advantageous to use what would suit your organisation and not try to make them fit.

Customer Value	Key Performance Indicators
Brand Loyalty	1. Increased sales per customer 2. The reduced onboarding cost for future sales
Customer Satisfaction	1. Increased Net Promoter Score 2. Increased positive feedback on social media platforms
Functional Benefit	1. Reduced waste in features/products (unused or not purchased) 2. Higher gross margin on products/services
Sale/Price	1. Increase sales/use 2. The increased price of product/service against industry inflation

Measuring the organisation's current state via the metrics above, the organisation can create outputs on a continuous improvement plan to test hypotheses and measure the impact of the change. Using the data from this study, leaders should identify and structure a pilot, create a vision to deliver value for an individual customer segment and continuously scale what works to the organisation. Once the objective has been met, the organisation can test greater involvement with the customer to see if the KPIs increase above the investment of the involvement. Finding internal customer representation can be a low-cost option to test greater customer involvement if metrics increase external customer involvement can be involved in the product cycle.

Internal Stakeholder Value

It it is a horrible rainy day in Auckland when Julie caught the

Uber to work. Walking in the rain, did not seem like an option with the typhoon blowing her windows shut earlier..

Even with the Uber, the short walk to the office escalator left Julie soaking wet, she hung up her umbrella and coat, grabbed a coffee and sat at her desk. "No Mark, no priority one and no meetings" she thought to herself. As she sipped her coffee and read through her 'urgent' emails, Julies teams call came through.

"Hey Julie, its Simon"
Although Julie could see Simon, she thought by the expression on his face, it was best not to point out the humour in what he just said.

"We have had so many priorities lately, I didn't realise we are coming up to our teams review, last year we had all new key performance indicators and I think we did well, however, you have been introducing new ways of thinking and I wanted to discuss our current performance indicators"

"Sure, I am free now, lets do it" Julie responded, truth be told, Julie hadn't even thought about performance indicators in the two months she had been at NZFX due to all the issues that had arisen.

Simon shared his screen to show the teams current KPIs.

As Julie stared at the KPIs, she stopped listening to Simon, she knew it was rude but she was busy reading the indicators
1. Total number of tickets completed vs raised
2. Percentage of uptime of the system
3. New Features launched
4. Efficiency
5. Time to resolve for P1-P5 issues
6. Number of agile ceremonies

"As you can see, each one of our key performance indicators is in green, trending the right way and similar to other business units" Simon finished

Julie must have looked shocked as Simon was looking uncomfortable

"Just so I am clear, our performance indicators are output driven, i.e the work we deliver and how we deliver it? We don't measure anything to do with our internal stakeholders or the impact on the customer?"

"We spoke about this on your first day, the whole country is our customer but really we mostly focus on our internal customers, I mean stakeholders. We can't measure value to them because we do not have full control on how we serve them, so we measure what we can control"

"I understand that Simon, the problem is, we do not know if we are maintaining our products sufficiently, we are not measuring the right things that ensure continuous improvement and if we focus on how we work, we won't know the impact of allocating more people to change projects".

"I am happy to change, but isn't it a bit late?"

"Never too late to measure the right things for the right reason. Customer value is what we really should be measuring but I agree, its a little hard to measure that within our area, since what we do helps the other departments serve the customers. We can edit it slightly and look at internal stakeholder value. Why not pop upstairs and we can discuss?"

Julie jumped up when Simon arrived and took him over to

the white board where she drew up the value chains that over lap around their team.

"As you can see we fit into these value chains, identifying them last time allowed us to bring together the right people, now we can use them to identify the appropriate stakeholders to measure."

"If we understand that customer value can be broken down into how satisfied and loyal a customer is, the benefit they consume and how often they purchase from us. We can translate this into how satisfied our stakeholders are, how often they contact us when they do not have to and the reduction in waste.

Customer Value	Stakeholder Value
Brand Loyalty	Product Loyalty
Price and Sales	Use of products
Customer Satisfaction	Stakeholder Satisfaction
Functional Benefit	Functional Benefit

"This makes sense" Simon analysed. "If we find measurements for these four areas, we will know how much value we are contributing to our stakeholders and thus if they are able to give more value to our customers? Would this help us prioritise as well?"

"Absolutely it will! If we know how much value we can provide to our stakeholders, we can understand how much time we should spend on maintenance, continuous improvement and change projects as well"

Internal Stakeholder Measures
"Ok, so lets start with Product Loyalty" Simon sat back down as if to say, please show me.

"The thought process around brand loyalty is that if we see more customers returning, we know they are choosing us more than our competitors, we also know that it costs less for each sale, because the Marketing spend isn't required.

From a customer point of view, this is the number of returning customers on a website, customers spending longer on the site or platform, customers login or turn up when asked, lower complaints and the sign up process is faster because we already know them and they know us.

Which means product loyalty could mean the number of complaints from our stakeholders? The difference between our stakeholders and customers is the fact they do not have much choice. Therefore, we can ascertain that if they are complaining, they are likely complaining to others about us and if given the chance, would move elsewhere.

Use of products on the other hand, goes hand in hand with loyalty. The percentage of time the users are using our system vs the total number of hours they are here at work? From a customer point of view, this would be measured as time on product, daily downloads and sales. i.e how much the customer is using or purchasing from us. However, for our internal stakeholders its purely use based, if we had more capital projects, we could use how much CAPEX funding they choose to give us, but we do not have that here."

Stakeholder Value	KPIs
Product Loyalty	Complaints
Use of products	Total use time
Stakeholder Satisfaction	
Functional Benefit	

"I don't think we have that many complaints though and our stakeholders should be using our systems all the time, shouldn't they be?" Simon frowned.

"In theory, yes, however, we know they have meetings and will likely use Microsoft products for certain functions of their jobs and as for complaints? How often do we record the number?"

"To be honest, I don't actually know where complaints are held and I've never measured hours of use before."

"Action on us then, can you go and get the data usage over the last year, lets break it down per department and I'll go look for the complaints register"

Simon went back to his desk while Julie went hunting for a complaint register. Or even a feedback register, which is just code for complaints.

Dear Managers,

After some time searching, I have noticed my team doesn't have a centralised feedback and improvements register (F&I), I would like to ensure we are meeting and exceeding your needs, can you please point me in the direction of any backlog you may have for us to work through.

Kind Regards,
Julie

'Much easier', Julie thought. Later that day it seemed her email didn't go as well as she thought. There was tens of emails coming through, all with different ideas of what the process was. Julie had been given at least four different backlogs of recommendations and two that had a list of complaints, absolutely not feedback, they were complaints.

Great thing was, after Julie placed all complaints, feedback and new features through sentiment analysis (which allows the computer to understand if it was negative, positive or neutral) she was able to create a graph of complaints over the last year by using the negative sentiments as a counter per month.

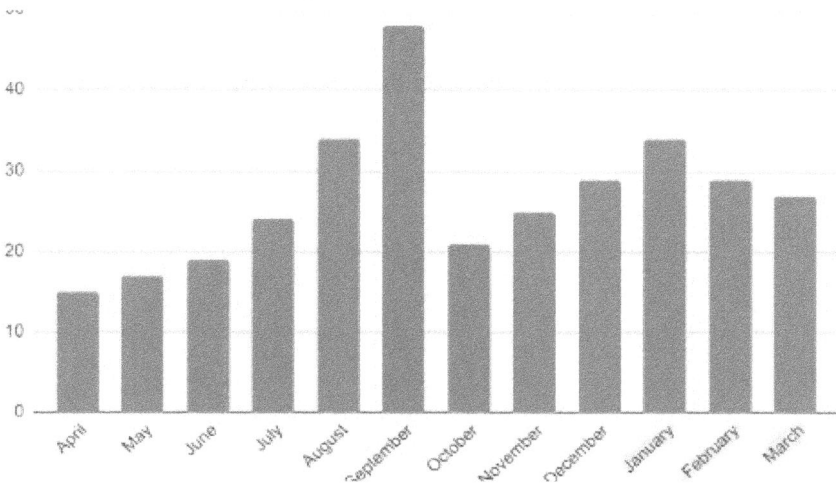

Julie also decided to highlight the three months she had been there, only to herself.

"Well that is interesting" Mark had popped out of no where.

He continued, once he knew he had made Julie jump. "So you are looking at brand loyalty through complaints?"

"That is correct, will call it product loyalty instead"

"Yes that makes sense, well, until we can ensure we measure the entire value chain together! Complaints were raising higher and higher under the last manager, thankfully have been decreasing since you have been here. I suspect that is because you have been running around including other departments in how you achieve results. Although, why the massive drop in September?"

"I have absolutely no idea. Are people happier here during October? Are there bonuses, I am unaware of?"

Julies screen pinged a chart from Simon just as Mark and Julie were looking at it.

Simon: I am a little shocked to be honest, it looks like we have seen a slow decline over the years in product use and whats worse, I am seeing a large drop off from two departments in October"

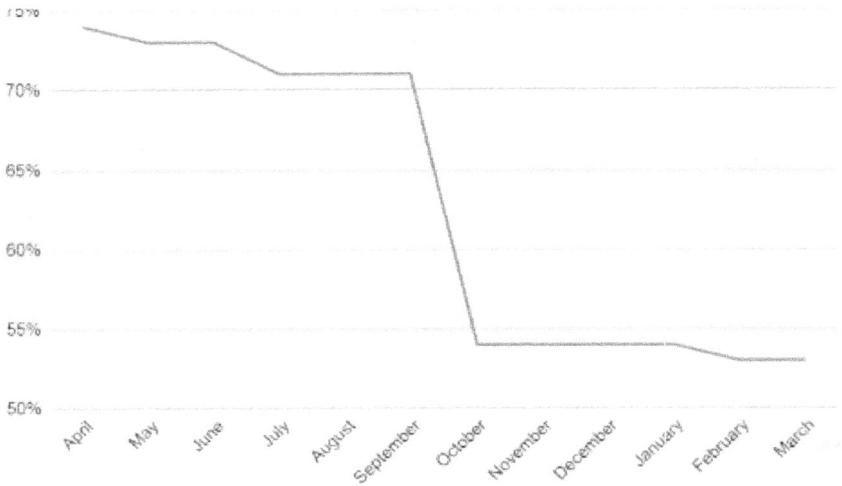

Julie: I am seeing some interesting complaint data at the same time, one moment, I'll overlay both.

Julie: The below columns are the number of negative complaints and the line is your data on usage.

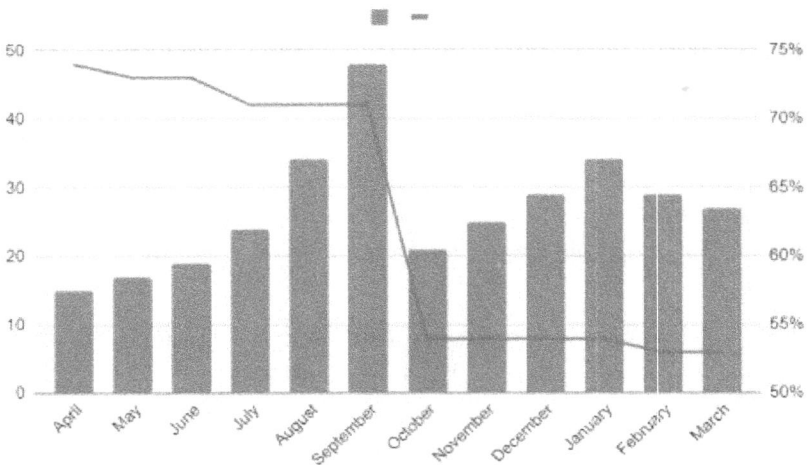

Simon: So the number of complaints increased until obviously those two departments started using different software for their delivery. This is dangerous Julie, we do not know what they are using, if they are using customer data, any security breaches or even if its costing NZFS a fortune!

Julie: I understand, the problem could be deeper though, if the complaints are not listened to, why would they support us. Now we are measuring, now we can support them better. Great work Simon, when you are ready, jump back up here and we can find our next KPIs.

"Wow thats great news Julie" Mark exclaimed, "I know it looks bad, but your data points combined under loyalty and use clearly show that departments feel its worth the risk going outside our tech department."

"My thoughts as well! If we take the average of the year, we can see we have an average of 27 complaints a month and an average of 63% usage of our products from all stakeholders. We have a starting place!

Stakeholder Value	KPIs	FY Measurement
Product Loyalty	Complaints	27
Use of products	Total use time	63%
Stakeholder Satisfaction		
Functional Benefit		

"Hey Julie, hey Mark. I see you have put the answers up. Thats product loyalty and use of products complete, leaving us functional benefit and stakeholder satisfaction remaining. "

"How do you want to do satisfaction, Julie?" Mark said with his hands folded

"Surely, we just ask everyone? Like a net promoter question?"

"No one ever answers those" Simon said before he realised he opened his mouth

"EXACTLY Simon, not only are surveys bias, because they can not be forced but they tend to only answer the question asked and not the question you want answered. You have already used a sentiment analysis to obtain the complaints, why not expand it to all communications to this department?"

"Thats brilliant Mark" Simon jumped up excited that its a technology solution. "If we read all emails, internal chat, forms and your new feedback process into a stakeholder sentiment analyser, we will be able to get a good rating of where we are at, it will also mean we can see the trend daily!"

"Ok that sounds fun Simon, why don't you see if you can get us the sentiment analysis over the last year? I'll work with Mark to figure out how we measure Functional benefit"

Simon nodded and headed back downstairs to work on the python script.

"For end customers, the functional benefit could be the emotional, financial and/or social. In our case Julie, I think its simpler than that. It is about waste in the system; everything your department does maintains a system that others use, continuously improves the system or changes the system for less waste"

"Mark, I think you are right, its just cleaner to say we should measure waste. Therefore, measure the value chain efficiencies. Yes we are only one part of the value chain, however, if our systems don't work, efficiency goes down and if they work better, it increases. I'll go through our software and see if I can track down the efficiency. This may take some time, I think we should measure efficiency at every part of the process. This means we need to measure how often there is value being added to the process vs the entire time the process had taken (cycle time)"

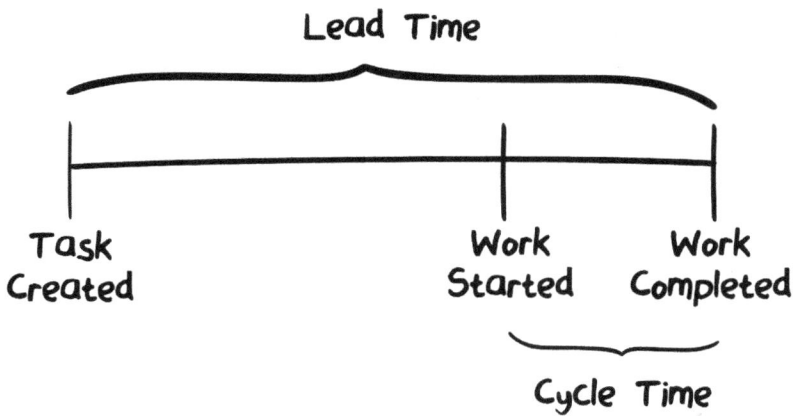

Lead Time

Task Created — Work Started — Work Completed

Cycle Time

"I think thats my time to leave, feel free to send me our teams efficiency score, if you come across it" Mark laughed and left Julie knowing he would actually obtain value from her measuring his team's efficiency.

Stakeholder Value	KPIs
Product Loyalty	Complaints
Use of products	Total use time
Stakeholder Satisfaction	Sentiment
Functional Benefit	Efficiency

Simon was able to calculate the current stakeholder sentiment analysis for the month within the hour. Going back over the year did take the rest of the day, Simon also warned Julie that it is likely to be less accurate then moving forward.

ANALYSIS

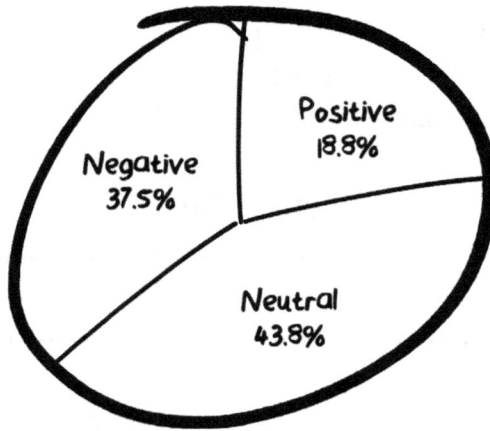

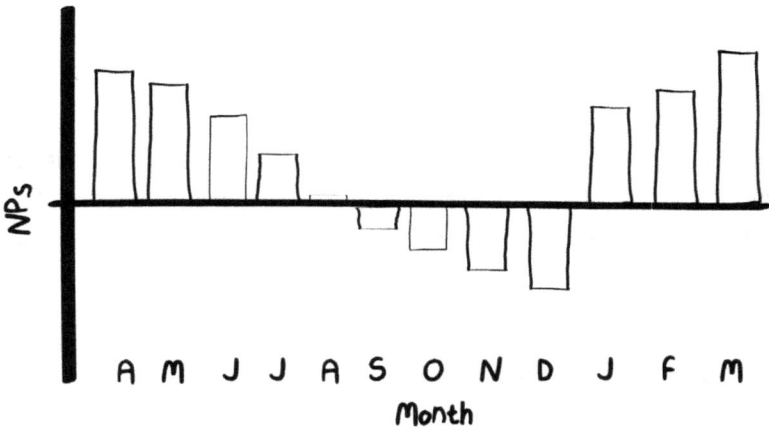

The net promoter score is created by subtracting negative feedback from positive and dividing across the total. In simple terms, you ignore the neutral and if you have more negative than positive, you have a negative percentage.

Another thing to note with net promoter scores is how you measure them, if completing manually, a score of 9 and 10 is positive, a score of 7 and 9 is neutral and a score of 0 to 6 is negative. This has been proven to remove bias.

Efficiency across the value chains however, took Julie until the end of the week. There was a lot of back dating Julie had to do. Firstly she had to reevaluate the value chains her teams had an impact on, then using their workflow tool and the front line's workflow tool, look at how often value added work was being completed vs how often valuable work was sitting in queues. The end result was not great news for NZFS.

At the start of last year, the efficiency of value delivered to the customer was 14%. This meant that there was 86% waste in the system. However, now there was an efficiency score of 11%, showing a 89% waste factor and a decrease in 3% efficiency across the organisation to the customer.

Stakeholder Value	KPIs	FY Measurement
Product Loyalty	Complaints	27
Use of products	Total use time	63%
Stakeholder Satisfaction	Stakeholder Analysis	18.75%
Functional Benefit	Efficiency	11%

Julie had finished the efficiency scores and placed all the documentation around a white board with the four key metrics in the middle.

On Monday she wanted to have a meeting with her team to see how they felt about the new KPIs.

"Have you met our GM of technology yet?"

Julie turned around to see Greg walking towards her, it was just after 8pm and Julie was not in the mood to meet someone else.

"Not yet, Hi Julie, its a pleasure to meet you. How are you settling in?"

It may have been because it was 8pm on a Friday evening, or the fact Julies babysitter had rung to say she can only stay until 8:30, but Julie had no idea who this lady was in front of her. As she shook her hand with this confident yet friendly co-worker, it clicked.

"Rhonda, I am fine thank you. Its been a fun ride so far, how was Australia?"

Rhonda is a 5ft 8 women in her 50's, immaculately dressed with short hair and a methodical approach to the way she talks. She had spent the last month over in Australia, negotiating with our partners over terms. Most importantly, she is the current Chief Executive Officer for NZFS.

"This looks interesting, walk me through your thinking, its obviously important as you are here so late"

"I would love to Rhonda. My team needs to know if what they are doing is impacting the customer, how much value do we provide for NZFS. We need a data driven way to determine if what we do is helping and therefore help us prioritise maintaining the products, continuously improving the products or changing them for new ones.

The previous KPIs focus on outputs that we achieve and how well we achieve them. They are judging what we do, what we were asked to do and not on the outcomes that our stakeholders and customers want.

We looked at our value maps, how NZFS delivers value to the customer and our part in that.

We know that customer value can be measured in a mixture of leading and lagging indicators. i.e what is measured before and after the sale. So we translated those metrics of customer value and created stakeholder value, how we help the front line deliver more value.

Loyalty is determined by complaints, how likely they would be to leave us if they had a choice. Use of our products in terms of a percentage, looking at how often departments make full use of our products. We used sentiment analysis, which is an automated tool, to see the trend of how our stakeholders see us. Lastly, we evaluated the efficiency score of our value chains, as a technology partner, we can have a rather large impact on the value chains efficiency."

Julie held her breathe, it wasn't quite rehearsed but she did mean to inform Greg at some stage.

"This is all well and good Julie, but we have robust KPIs that we complete at the executive level" Greg started while Rhonda was reading the white board.

"Creating your own KPIs is not what we do here at NZFS, I would appreciate it if you would stick to the previous approved KPIs and then we can discuss iterations, I mean, we are Agile here at Technology NZFS!"

Rhonda was silent, she had read the summary on the white board and to Greg's rant about authority.

"Can I clarify something please Julie?"

"Of course" Julie said

"These KPIs are not about you and your team, but about how you work with the entire organisation?"

"Thats correct, we are all working on the same mission"

"I really like the value maps, it makes it a lot easier to see how value is delivered to our customers without the blur of functional hierarchies. You have found that two departments have stopped using your products, how does that make you feel?"

"Horrible, they are breaking the rules, they know they would be but the service must be so bad that they would rather risk it then carry on"

"I shall take this up with Henry!' Greg stipulated when he realised it was the Marketing department.

"I would rather you not Greg, what Julie has done with these KPIs is to automatically signal to her and her team if they are thrilling their stakeholders. If they are not, then things need to change. Julie, do you need any funding for this or can this be internal?" said Rhonda, almost ignoring Greg.

"I have all the resources and capabilities to keep this up to date, it'll also be automated and delivered as part of our technology meeting once a month."

"Great, I do not believe you require my approval, but you have my support. It would be great Greg, if something similar was to be done for all of technology, then we would know what impacts the rest of the business is having with changes made in technology. Putting this into your data transformation strategy would help. I am also interested in how we measure success at NZFS, we currently focus on return on equity, however, it lags years behind, meaning we only know if we are successful today, years after we have made the decision. I would like to know of ways we can anticipate customer value"

Rhonda took several photos of the whiteboard and asked for a copy of the customer value metrics to be emailed to her. As Rhonda and Greg left, Julie knew on Monday, Greg would be frustrated, but its 8:30pm and its home time.

Seven Circumstances of Strategy

Fixed Constraints

The weekend was filled with fun as Julie and her children went to the beach and had dinner at the SkyTower. For the first time in two months, things were falling into place at Julie's workplace, NZFS. It was surprising for her to realize how much her work affected her home life. The concept of work-life balance is intriguing because it implies that work-related stress shouldn't affect one's home life.

Monday morning was unexpectedly filled with a meeting with the technology leadership team that lasted for one hour. The meeting was held in the boardroom, indicating that it was important.

"Morena Team," Greg said with a mixture of authority and excitement. Julie thought to herself, "This can't be good. There was nothing in the papers or any news over the weekend. I thought there were no major releases, and we're nearing the end of the financial year. Oh no."

"In less than a month, we'll start our next financial year, but with all the events that have occurred over the last month, we haven't had the time to prepare ourselves, which means we're now behind in getting approval for next year's budgets. Patrick from the PMO has informed me that finance wants our business cases ready for approval by the end of the week," Greg said.

"You've got to be kidding me," Mark exclaimed, expressing the thoughts of everyone in the room. Julie, who hadn't yet begun looking at her budget requirements, joined in the protest. "It's not possible for everyone to complete satisfactory business cases in a week, let alone prioritize them," she said.

Greg stood up from his seat, placing his hands on the back of the leather chair. "My next piece of news might make things easier then. Our budget this year as a technology group will be 50% of last year's budget," he announced, causing shock and silence in the room. "Yes, it's not what we all would want, but due to an audit from finance, we were unable to show the return on equity we promised last year and this year we're likely to be negative due to the cost of the modular program.

The good news is that everyone we have now, we can still afford, it just means no additional contractors and no vendors for this financial year. We will do everything in-house. If we can't achieve our expectations with that budget, we will need to perform another restructuring to lower our headcount."

Furthermore, Greg added that the company CEO has changed the direction of the company's key performance indicators (KPIs).

"Rhonda has spoken to the board about how we measure success here at NZFS and although return on equity is very important to the company, the risk of measuring this year's after delivery is too much risk for NZFS in this market. Therefore, she has implemented customer-centric KPIs throughout the executive teams. Our strategic initiatives must show how they align to one or more of the KPIs and thus show how it increases or maintains customer value."

"Personally, I find this new way forward quite refreshing, it does mean, however, we can not just use the business cases from last year and just 'roll them over."

Customer Value	KPIs
Brand Loyalty	• Sales per customer • Onboarding cost per customer
Price and Sales	• Return on Equity • Increase profit against industry inflation
Customer Satisfaction	• Brand sentiment • Positive feedback
Functional Benefit	• Reduced waste to customer Higher gross margin

Almost all of these metrics will be live data run out of technology for the whole company to see. Brand loyalty, measured by sales per customer and onboarding cost per customer, shows that it costs us less in marketing to obtain new customers because our current customers recommend us and continue using us for all their needs. Price and Sales are standard with our ROE, with an additional KPI to measure our market share adjusted profit, taking into account the industry's rises and falls.

Customer satisfaction will be measured through sentiment analysis of data and analytics, looking through social media, phone calls, emails, and anywhere our customers are talking about us. Functional benefit is all about obtaining more value for our customers at a lower cost, or in this year's budget, a fixed cost. We can measure and show these through productivity and efficiency gains.

The executive team worked very hard on these KPIs over the weekend, and I think you'll all agree, they help shape our strategic initiatives," Greg concluded.

Julie couldn't believe he could sit there with a straight face and say he helped create those KPIs, she was biting her lip as she thought to herself. "So as we are an agile organisation, let's take this financial year in that thought process. We have fixed capacity, now how do we plan a year's worth of work that maximizes the customer value KPIs?" Greg sat back into his chair, after what he thought was an inspiring speech about the customer and performance.

The table looked like they had been slapped by a wet fish. This isn't what the technology team were used to, they would normally have hundreds of good ideas with loose business cases, make them look like they will be complete, obtain budget, and then spend the year outsourcing to vendors.

"I know I've only been here for two months," Julie finally broke the silence, "but I do have a solution we could try. Creating output-based strategic initiatives like 'go to the cloud' and 'ability for modular deployments' are all great ideas, but the future is uncertain, our customers are complex, and the market is shifting beneath us. Putting this level of planning into a business case would only work in a complicated environment, i.e., one that doesn't have multiple variations in the solution[81].

We have done the work, we now have our value chains, we

know how work is completed from start to the end customer across the organisation, however, we haven't had a workshop on setting strategy, better yet, we haven't moved from static strategy planning to adaptive strategy.

Adaptive strategy will allow us to pivot if the data says we should, it allows us to reduce waste by not completing business cases up front, and it moves with our customers, not our products."

"I for one would prefer not to spend a week doing business cases that either won't get approved or are set up for failure," Mark chimed in, he genuinely didn't want to write any more documents.

"We have a vision and a set of KPIs to work off of, if we come together tomorrow for a day, we can create an adaptive strategy that will allow us an operating model with agility built in. By tomorrow, we can create high-level objectives, together, as a team, that allow us to show what we will achieve for this year. We will request funding for the WHAT we will achieve and draw down that funding on the HOW later."

"Sounds risky," Alex, the CISO, spoke up, "although if we build enough constraints into these objectives, it could work. It would also mean my team wouldn't need to do a security assessment on initiatives that may or may not be completed. Can you expand more on adaptive strategy and objectives for me?"

"Good point, Alex," Julie said. "Yes, we will save time this week, and our teams will reduce waste throughout the process as well. I have two models we could use.

The Seven Circumstances of Strategy is a simple yet effective set of questions to ask yourself as a delivery team. 'Why are we here? Who do we serve? Where do we play? How will we win? In what way will we deliver? And when will we know we are success-ful?' These questions are in that order on purpose. Think of it like a pyramid. If one answer to a question changes, the items up the pyramid must also change to accommodate. It allows you to con-tinuously validate your assumptions on each question and know what needs to change if one question differs."

Julie stood up and drew a big triangle on the whiteboard to illustrate her point.

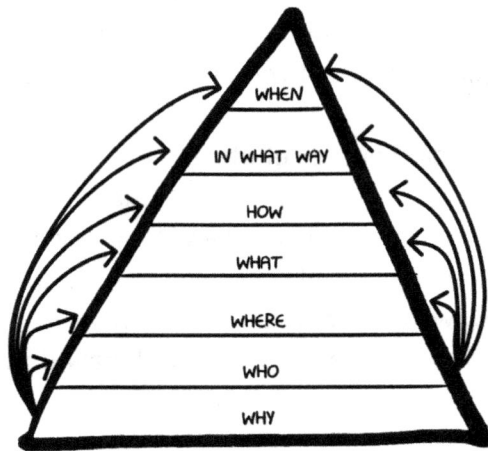

"This guides us through our decision-making process and keeps us aligned as a team. The other model which I believe we can use alongside the Seven Circumstances is the Triple O model - Objectives, Outcomes, and Outputs. It helps us to focus on what we want to achieve, what results we expect, and what actions we will take to achieve them."

Triple O Model

"The idea is that as a group we decide on the objectives. We may have separate outcomes that we create that help achieve the objective, but an outcome is just a hypothesis. We believe the outcome will help us achieve an objective, but if it doesn't, we pivot as quickly as we can to the next outcome, again reducing waste.

"How does this differ from an Objective and Key Results (OKRs) Julie?" Alex asked.

"OKRs are great at an organisation level. They are designed to be multi-year SMART goals. Specific, measurable, attainable, realistic and timely goals. They tend to be implemented incorrectly, either there are hundreds of them, so they are too easy to obtain or companies have multiple levels of OKRs, losing focus.

OKRs are meant to be set at an organisation layer, showing us all what the top objectives and key outcomes are. We cannot control the rest of the organisation, however, we can control what we can do. Strategic initiatives are in theory outcomes to the organisation as well, which are great again if we had OKRs set up top. But we are by ourselves, so I recommend focusing on our sphere of influence.

What I like about the triple O model is that it simplifies delivery. It's not business as usual, that's a fixed constraint we need to work out. It's not continuous improvement, that's what reduces the cost of business as usual in order to achieve more change.

The triple O model is a change-focused approach that prioritises yearly objectives that are SMART goals that can be completed within a year. These objectives are supported by a set of outcomes that are continually delivered until the objective is met. To keep the focus on short-term experiments that yield fast results, outcomes should be no longer than 90 days and should be delivered to customers, not internal stakeholders.

The outputs are the building blocks for the outcome. Outcomes are for the customer, while outputs can be for customers, internal stakeholders, or partners. These outputs are delivered by teams and help deliver the outcome to the customer. Ideally, outputs should be delivered within a week, although some may have two-week sprints. However, the duration and composition of outputs should not be decided upon by technology leaders,

Greg frowned "Then who should be deciding the outputs for our people??"

"Great point Greg, it is the people. The people doing the work know how to achieve the outcome best. So it is normally them that decide which outputs, with our input of course.

Lastly tomorrow we should all decide on a common framework for delivery, we have made some great changes without going through the process change committee and I believe we can set ourselves up for success next year, if we do."

Julie paused, she didn't mean to sell her ideas, she just wanted to take advantage of the situation. Moments passed and all but one person was keen. Very surprised, Julie set up a workshop on her phone there and then, before people could change their mind. Inviting everyone from the technology leadership team, except Greg who had an urgent meeting to go to.

Seven Circumances of Strategy
Julie spent the entirety of Monday preparing for Tuesday's workshop. She wanted to ensure that everything was perfect.

She arrived at the meeting room thirty minutes early, at 8:00am, and was pleased to find Mark already there.

"I'm so excited!" Mark exclaimed as he greeted Julie.
"I'm so worried," replied Julie, her nerves showing.

"Don't worry," Mark reassured her. "You're giving them a solution to their problem. Harry from digital already told me how happy he is. He delivered no customer value this year and has been struggling to complete any business cases of value for next year."

"That's even more worrying," said Julie. "Now they think we'll solve all their issues! All we're doing is finding a way around the timings. Although, I am secretly hoping we can move some of our items to orange and focus on outcomes and productivity now that Rhonda has pushed the customer value metrics."

Everyone started arriving early, which was a good sign. Usually, the technology leaders would drift in ten minutes late, as if their time was somehow more important than everyone else's. But not today. Everyone came in five minutes early, coffees in hand and mostly with a smile on their faces.

"Kia Ora team, today we are going to go through the seven circumstances of strategy. Its an adaptive strategy model that tells us when and how to adapt our strategy, based on the new data points or failed assumptions we come up against. As you have heard me say before, we will come up against changes, we have employees, technology and customers. All three are complex. We need to probe, sense a response and then respond properly."

Julie drew a large pyramid on the whiteboard and began to explain the different levels. "At the base of the pyramid, we have the 'Why' - this is our purpose or the reason we exist. Next, we have

'Who' - this is the customer or user we are serving. Then, we have 'Where' - this is the market or industry we operate in. Following that, we have 'How' - this is the unique value proposition or approach we take. 'In What Way' - this is the business model or delivery method we use. And finally, 'When' - this is the timeline or milestones for success.

"It's important to note that each level of the pyramid is interconnected and dependent on the levels above it. If one level changes, it will affect the levels above it. By continuously validating our assumptions and understanding how each level of the pyramid is impacted, we can quickly adapt our strategy as needed."

The group listened intently, nodding along as Julie spoke. "I know this might sound daunting, but it's a simple and effective way to stay aligned and make decisions as a team. By understanding and utilizing the 7 C's, we can better navigate the complexities of our organisation, employees, technology, and customers."

Our mission at NZFS is delivering great customer service with sincerity, pride and innovation!"

WHY do we exist: Julie drew the companies vision up on the whiteboard. "This is NZFS's why, we are a customer centric organisation and we deliver great service.

Not everyone will agree with this vision but it is not for us to debate today, we need this to be our foundation. Remember if our WHY changes, everything changes!"

WHO do we serve: "Can anyone answer this question?"

Laughs were plenty with guesses for who we serve, apart from Mark who looked insulted that no one seemed to have any knowledge around our customer personas. The standard comment was that we serve all of New Zealand.

"Very funny everyone. I have just messaged everyone links to Marks customer segmentations and the value chains we completed last month. Lets work through this information and focus on the niche segmentation we wish to serve, not the industry or everyone."

To illustrate the point, Julie drew a funnel showing the different types of customer groups from everyone to an individual.

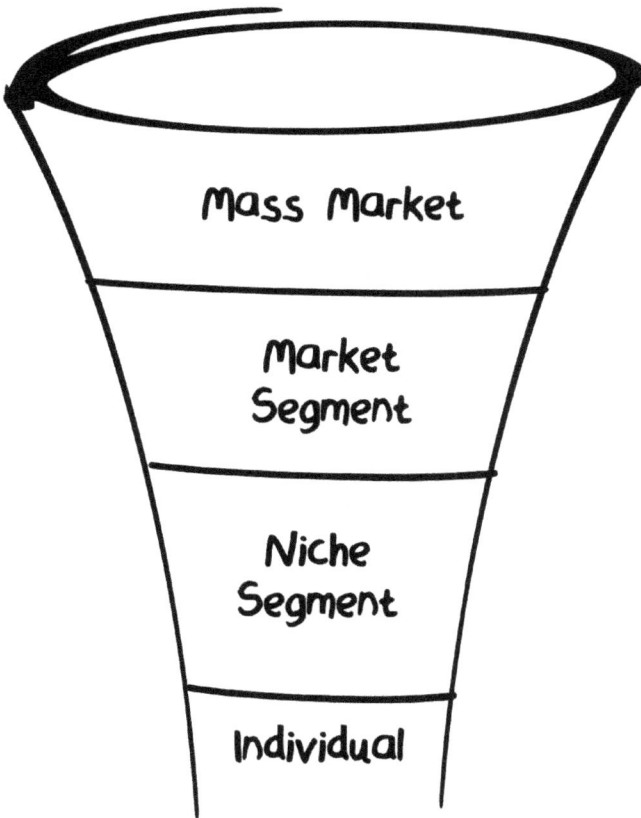

There was acceptance that niche customer segmentation makes sense. If we focus on one group, we will likely hit other groups, however, if we try to serve everyone, we will please no one. Mark was keen to go down to an individual level, no one else was though. It was too much of a jump for the team, but they did agree to give each niche customer segmentation a real name.

The customer section took over two hours and another coffee round. Ending on five customers the technology leadership from NZFS believed they served. There was:

1. John the self employed man from Dunedin
2. Sharon the property tycoon from Auckland
3. Sandra the mom property owner from Wellington
4. Charles the wealthy investor from Queenstown and
5. Brad the young male from Hamilton.

Recognition of the fact that multiple internal stakeholders and partners have played a role in addressing these customer issues, with a clear understanding that ultimately, the customer is the end recipient.

Over lunch Julie asked Simon if he could give a return from each one of these segments. Simon said it'll be easy and be in Julies teams chat by the end of lunch.

"Welcome back team, Simon decided to help us prioritise and sent us some data from the last five years. The average return from each of our chosen customer segmentations"

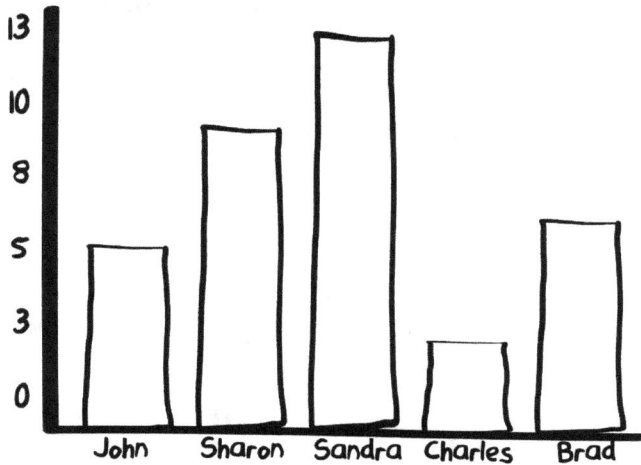

Chart with y-axis values: 13, 10, 8, 5, 3, 0
Bars labeled: John, Sharon, Sandra, Charles, Brad

"As you can see, Sandra is our top-performing customer and Charles is our least profitable. This information helps us prioritize different customers in the future. It's crucial to remember that who we serve is just as important as our overall mission or purpose. These customers align with our values and goals, otherwise they wouldn't be our customers. However, if we shift our focus to a different customer, it may require us to adjust our approach or target market."

WHERE do we play? "We have already touched on where, we know we only work in New Zealand and our value chains are the following:

1. Retail - Sharon
2. Lending - Sandra
3. Digital & Cards - Brad
4. Wealth - Charles
5. Business Banking - John

The team looked at the return from each value chain, you could tell this was the first time the leaders had realised there was such a dramatic difference between customer segmentations.

"I want to start with Sandra if thats ok, she is our most valuable customer and a good example for our next step.

Agility Delivery Canvas

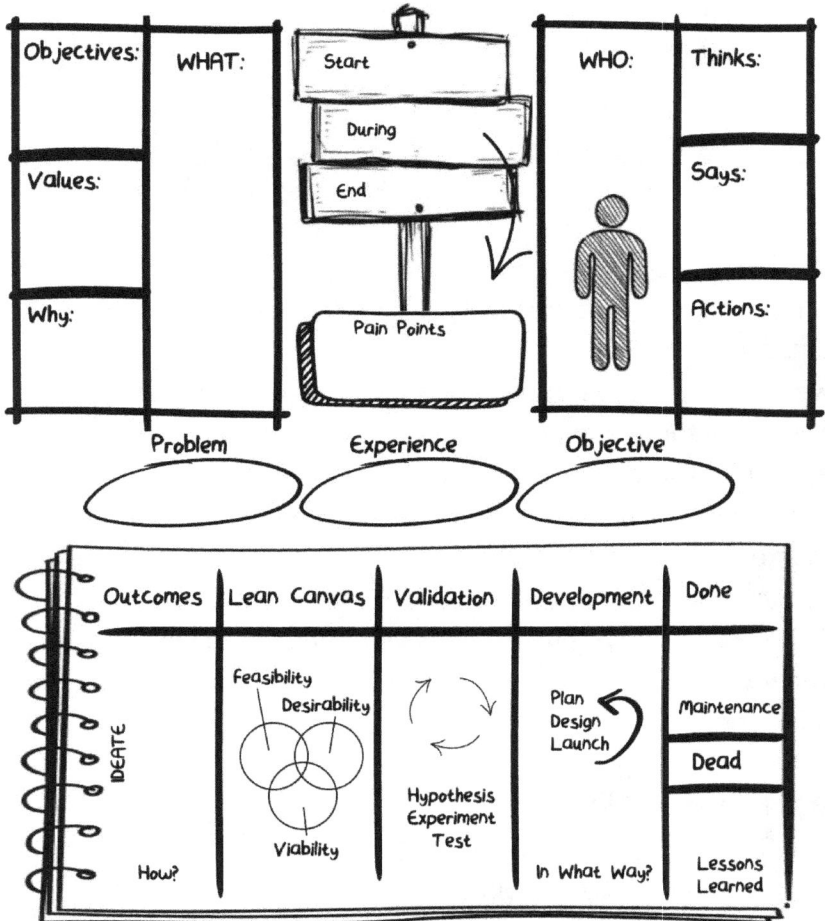

"I want to introduce you to the Agility Delivery Canvas or AcDC" Julie looks around for smiles, but everyone was too busy evaluating the canvas that they hadn't noticed.

"Each customer should end up with one or more of these canvases, one per objective. It allows anyone to see everything on a single A0 sheet. It is a constant reminder of the Why, Who, Where, What on the top of the canvas, with a more dynamic How along the bottom. We have the value map for Sandra as its the same one for lending, however, we need to decide as a team where we focus

Simon has sent you complaints for each segment over the last year."

"It's clear that Sandra's biggest problem is the length and complexity of the mortgage process," Harry said, standing up. "Which I agree with. It currently takes six weeks to get a mortgage approval and goes through fourteen different people for approval."

The team created a high-level customer journey map for Sandra around this problem and identified the key problem being the time and effort required to obtain a mortgage.

"Although this is great, isn't it the same with our competitors?" Alex asked, looking deflated.

"Yes, I agree, Alex. So, if we can find a way to solve this for Sandra, we would have a competitive advantage. It's a positive step forward!"

"So now we know our organisational Why, we know we're focusing on Sandra who wants a fluid customer experience on the customer journey map of obtaining a mortgage, with the pain point being that it's slow and cumbersome. As you can imagine, if we changed the customer journey map to focus on another journey, our pain point would be different, which means our objective would be different as well."

What Problem are we Solving: "We have touched on the problem and experience Sandra needs already; a problem statement is one thing, now we need to give ourselves an objective. A SMART goal.

Our Vision is on going, our objectives need to be yearly. So what objective can we create that helps us focus on Sandra getting a mortgage and relieve her pain?"

"Can I confirm that Objectives don't encompass maintaining our current value; that its new?" Mark already knew the answer, but Julie answered, because it was a good question.

"Correct Mark, maintenance or business as usual, is a constraint on our ability to achieve change. These objectives ARE the change."

Objective 1 - Sandra - Achieve a five-day turnaround for mortgage approval with minimal contact with frontline workers, utilising digital platforms and automation to streamline the process.

It didn't take the team long to come up with their first objective. Julie felt proud of her team's work, as the new approach not only simplified the delivery process but also helped to focus everyone on an objective that they knew the customer wanted. Although it would have been ideal to gather input from real customers, the team was able to use real-life customer data to create their objectives.

As the day came to a close, the team had successfully established four objectives. They had combined John and Charles' objectives as they wanted similar things and Charles wasn't as important as the others. In just one day, the technology leadership team was able to shift their focus from having hundreds of outcomes to honing in on just four objectives, streamlining their approach and increasing efficiency.

Objective 2 - Sharon - Make information easily accessible to customers through branch, online, and mobile platforms, ensuring consistency and quick response times to inquiries.

Objective 3 - Brad - Improve customer convenience by integrating a marketplace for partners to provide additional services directly through customer accounts. This will allow customers to easily access all of their bank and non-bank accounts, including crypto-currency accounts, in one convenient location.

Objective 4 - John & Charles - Combine business, wealth and retail banking into a seamless platform, providing business banking clients with the same services and products as retail customers. This includes the integration of a marketplace for partners to add their services to customer accounts, giving customers the ability to easily access all bank and non-bank accounts, including crypto.

How will we deliver: With our objectives in place, we can now begin to develop our solutions. The HOW section of the AcDC model will guide us in creating efficient and effective ways to achieve our objectives. Remember, an outcome is just a hypothesis that it will achieve our desired objective. It's important to stay flexible and adapt our solutions as needed.

To ensure that we don't increase waste, the first step is to bring together everyone who serves the customer within the customer journey. For us, this may not be practical. As an alternative, I recommend that we hold design sessions with one representative from each team, spanning the entire business. We will use design thinking to generate ideas and prioritize them based on their perceived value to the customer and alignment with our objectives.

They all start on the left hand side on the AcDC in ideation. There is a work in progress limit in the next column; it ensures that we only focus on a small number of these at a time. It is to analyse the outcomes feasibility, desirability, and viability in a lean canvas, you can see more information about the lean canvas here: https://leanstack.com/lean-canvas.

The idea behind the lean canvas is to condense long and tedious business cases onto a single A3 sheet that includes all the necessary information for making a decision. It is a constantly evolving document that is updated with new information that may prompt the need to abandon an outcome. The main objective of this column is to assess the feasibility, desirability, and viability of the outcome.

Each lean canvas should have a set of assumptions and hypotheses to test. You may have several of these in progress at any given time. You are testing these hypotheses with customers, collecting data, and validating that the benefits will actually be realised by investing in the change. From my experience, it is at this stage that most outcomes are moved to the "dead" column.

Only once the outcome is deemed ready, should teams be allowed to work on it. This will save weeks of paperwork and approval and will also reduce the risk of failure"

"Great plan Julie, I would like my security and risk people to be involved in the lean canvas, if thats ok?" Alex looked worried

"Absolutely Alex, we need key members from the value chain to be part of the lean canvas development, and if you find anything that puts a stop to it, its a good thing, it means we haven't wasted time and resources!

In What Way will we deliver: Depending on our solutions to our objectives, we may need a different framework for delivery. This is why the arguments about waterfall vs agile are mute. With Agility, we choose the delivery mechanism that makes the most sense for the environment and the outcome."

"I think you're going to say it anyway, Julie," Mark laughed.

"Thanks, Mark. To ensure we make it easy for PMO, finance, and ourselves, I recommend we move our teams to a 90-day strategy. They pull the outcome of the highest priority, break it down into outputs, and deliver what they can in 90 days. Preferably, our outcomes are no bigger than 90 days."

"This allows our teams to be empowered to make critical decisions that they know the most about and allows us to take a step up and look at the overall delivery of the quarter."

"I believe we would end up with more visibility this way, instead of waiting on each other with multiple backlogs. We would have four backlogs combined on our workflow tool, already prioritized by the objective. We will all work together to get the most value out the door each quarter."

"I think it's sold, Julie," Harry laughed. Everyone was in agreement, but Julie obviously wasn't expecting it.

When will we deliver: "Lastly, if our framework changes, the only thing that would be impacted is when. We need to consider how we will measure success and what lead indicators will help us know we are on the right track during the quarter. I recommend linking customer KPIs directly into PowerBI so we can see them as we release outcomes, creating a dynamic roadmap that allows us complete visibility for the rest of the year. Additionally, we should let the teams decide their own reporting requirements to help them deliver the outputs.

Everyone nodded in agreement. It might have been because it was now 4:30pm in New Zealand, which is usually hometime. Regardless, Julie got the decision she wanted: agreement for the use of objectives, outcomes, and outputs, a new way of creating a strategy that continuously updates if the elements of the strategy change, printing the AcDC for each objective for all to see, introducing 90 day strategies, and creating dynamic roadmaps for long-term adaptive planning.

The technology leadership team worked together to expand on the objectives with success criteria before the end of the week. Each success criteria increased one or more customer values by a significant margin based on customer input. Patrick from PMO and Finance accepted the "business cases," but were suspicious of how they were going to achieve these measurements.

Julie mitigated their concerns by making them the gatekeepers to draw down change funding each quarter. This actually suited Julie. 60% of the current budget would be allocated at the start of the year to maintain technology products and services, with 40% drawn down throughout the year based on the outcomes the technology department aimed to achieve.

Greg, on the other hand, pretended not to know what was going on. Julie suspected this was to allow him deniability in case things went wrong and the ability to say that his leadership led to such extreme wins. He did give one piece of advice, which Julie found both annoying and negotiable. He suggested that the technology department be split into four, with each objective assigned to a specific team, not by function, but teams would only focus on one objective.

Although Julie liked the idea, it wasn't something she had discussed with her peers. It wasn't a restructure of roles, but it would mean a restructure of work.

Design Studio

"Kia Ora everyone" Julie stood before 24 individuals from across the customer service teams who were asked to arrive with only two days' warning. It was a Thursday, and the technology department was completing their first 90-day strategy session the following week, but they had nothing to work on yet.

"I have asked you all here to bring your ideas to help us achieve an objective for Sandra, our fictional customer persona. She wants us to 'achieve a five-day turnaround for mortgage approval with no contact with front-line workers', and you represent the valuable knowledge we have from the end-to-end customer journey," said Julie.

Many of the people in the room had already been involved in a session with Julie, so they were quite excited. Mark, Harry, and Alex were at the back of the room, and you could tell there was a mixture of excitement and worry on their faces.

"We will be doing a two-hour sprint called 'Design Studio'. The idea is to get as many concepts up on the wall as fast as possible. No idea is a bad idea; you represent your teams, and you know the current pains and opportunities.

I want to see everyone raising ideas, concepts and improvements, I want to see active discussion and good feedback. By the end of today's session, we will have a prioritized list of outcomes that is something we can deliver to the customer, measure, and help us obtain the objective. Since this session focuses on technology, let's take note of any non-technology related ideas on the other side of the room, so you can bring them to the attention of your teams. Does that sound fun?

Step 1: "We will split into teams of 5 and 6, ensuring there is a mix of roles and experience."

Step 2: "I want you to take a piece of paper and draw two lines so that you create four spaces. You all have five minutes to think of four concepts that help achieve the objective, ready... steady.... GO!"

Julie looked around the room like a school teacher and was amazed at how different everyone was, some people were drawing characters, some writing stories, others were completing process diagrams and then their was the technologists who were doing system designs.

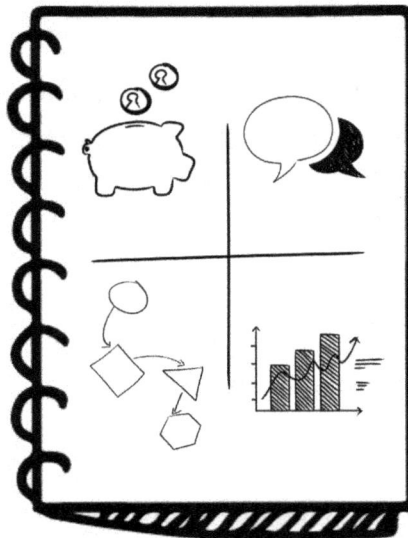

Step 3: "Times Up! Stop drawing" Everyone laughed, they may have been uncomfortable at the start but now they were cheating, trying to finish. "The time constraints are on purpose, not just so we can get out of here on time, but also because it increases innovation. Now everyone may have between one and four concepts.

I want everyone to spend one minute presenting their concepts to their group and then one minute for the group to ask clarifying questions. The idea around clarifying questions is that you are not judging, you are merely filling in the gaps between their presentation and your understanding. You have fifteen minutes in total for this activity; go!"

Step 4: "Awesome job everyone, how did that go?" Julie listened to laughter and feedback on the illustrations, some were acting it out, others read but they all enjoyed the feedback. "Now we are going to repeat the process, you have heard what others have said, I want you to polish off your concepts, remember its ok to steal other peoples ideas or to completely change your own! You have five minutes, go!"

The sudden new rules around stealing made many people get up and look around, they were combining ideas, scrapping ideas and creating completely new ideas, all within the five minutes allocated.

Step 5: "Now you have another fifteen minutes to present to each other again. One minute pitch, one minute of probing questions. Probing questions are where you are trying to get more detail. Go!"

Step 6: "Nicely done everyone, I hope you enjoyed it. Now as a group I want you to put all the ideas up on the wall. Use scissors to cut them out, blue tak on the back and up on the wall. I want each member of your team to grab three green sticker dots. I want you to vote three times, but there are rules.

1. You can not vote for your own
2. You can vote as many times as you like on one item, as long as you have dots remaining
3. You can not change your mind

I want you then to prioritise your ideas from highest votes to lowest. Your highest ranked idea will be the one you will present to everyone. So once you have chosen your number one, you have fifteen minutes to plan how to pitch. It can be theatrical, story telling, death by power point or however you think best. Everyone understand? Good, let's go!"

The four groups didn't take long to decide their favourites, one group combined two ideas to make a super idea. What surprised Julie was two of the teams started building props to act out their changes.

Step 7: The groups spent 10 minutes presenting their ideas and 10 minutes of questions. At the end of each pitch, each person was asked what they WISHED the pitch had, what they WONDERED if the pitch should have and what they LIKED about the pitch ,on a post-it note.

"Well done team, we have had four great pitches and you have all received great questions and feedback on your post-it notes. I want you to spend the last few moments tidying up your concept and place them over on the ideate column on the AcDC canvas. On your way out, I want you all to vote for one, again, it can not be yours. This will give us our priority on which outcome we will start on first. Thank you again."

The teams started to vacate the workshop room, sticking their red dot on the way out. It was a clear order.

Outcome 1: Customers can apply for a mortgage online with all the necessary information and documents for the mortgage advisers to complete the application process, so that a prelim result can be emailed.

What Julie liked about this outcome was that it was simple. The customer would get the experience they require, instead of being forced to ring up, they could complete the application on their computer or phone, upload the documents and then NZFS would do its standard backend process. We will look good on the outside, which was a good step one.

The rest of Thursday and Friday was just as fun; different outcomes were created for all four objectives, ideas were raised for other departments, which teams took with them. The technology leaders agreed to split their teams across the four objectives. Yes it meant that they will have all four in flight, but it was a good compromise with Greg.

The business analysts took the outcomes from the lean canvas section, created a stakeholder matrix, which showed who was involved and how they were impacted; they worked on the benefit realisation of each and lastly got rough calculations of the people costs it would take.

NZFS technology didn't have time to complete througher validation, there was a two day turnaround on four outcomes to be validated with the customers and any assumptions checked. Susan from Julies team raised a good point. We can use the validation phase to work out what can and can not be validated prior to work beginning. Then if the assumptions are proven incorrect during development, pull the plug. Julie thought this was a great idea and would mean we do not have to slow down.

"Talk about just in time delivery Julie" said Mark

"Its 4pm on Friday Mark, this is an early finish for us" Julie smiled. "We have the first 90 day strategy session booked for objective one on Tuesday. It'll be about 60 of us working on the first outcome. Then we repeat each day there after. Should be good"

"Julie, we have completely changed how work comes to the team, we now have customer requirements and if the teams really can delivery these outcomes, we would be delivering new functionality to the customer in 90 days, as oppose to three years! I think you deserve to be happy."

It was that moment that Julie really understood what she and her team had done. It started off with just measuring where they are and some minor changes to remove leadership pain points. Now they are about to embark on NZFS first step towards agility. Something the employees and the customers want. Julie left work at 4:30pm, not only was this earlier than normal, but she went home happier then she has been in eight weeks.

90 day strategy

Delivery Rhythme

A sunny Monday morning in Auckland city can not be beaten (unless you were in Whanganui; New Zealands most beautiful city), today however, Julie and the rest of the leaders were heading upto E drive, the hub on the northshore of Auckland.

Greg didn't want to spend too much on the 90 day strategy experiment and the only way we could get everyone together without travel costs, was to use E drive. E drive was mostly a technology hub, full of developers, servers and COBOLT developers. Most people in NZFS can not remember what COBOLT is, though some call it COBOL. Actually they might be right Julie thought. Without those developers, apparently we fall into a financial collapse with zombies and terminators. Or so the story goes.

"Welcome to E drive Julie." Mark popped up, just as Julie got through security.

"Do you track me with a GPS Mark?"

"Absolutely. Its your work phone, it lets me know when you are near."

Julie couldn't quite tell if Mark was serious, however, that phone is now being turned off at weekends Julie thought to herself.

"I have a question before we set up for the 90 day strategy session. We were able to easily prioritise the outcomes because we only had a small amount, we used dot voting which I obviously love, but what do we do if there was hundreds of ideas?"

"Great question Mark" Julie walked Mark over to the ping pong table where there was a white board. "We will need to include a rhythm to our framework, one where everyone knows the cut-off deadlines. We need to create the objectives yearly and have a constant flow of new outcomes assigned to the objectives with cut off points for delivery."

"Something like this?" Mark pulled out an A2 sized picture of the year in a big circle, sectioned into four delivery phases and the deadlines for each part of the process. On the other side was a more detailed timing map for the quarter itself.

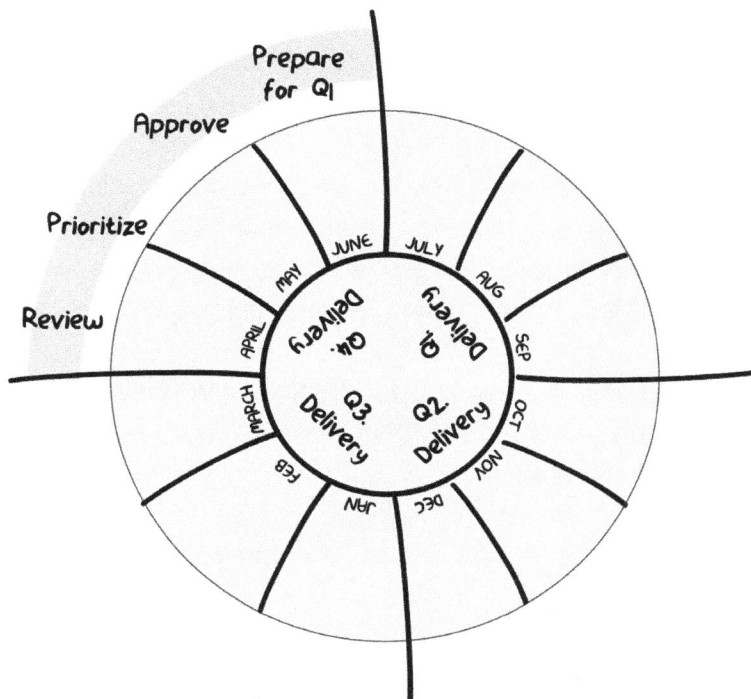

"Mark that is amazing, did you do that over the weekend?" Julie was impressed, it allows a simple reflection of the process without missing any key dates

"Yes I knew if we wanted to make this stick, we would need to start focusing on a brand, print outs, I think we should bring everything under the NZFS colours as well, rather than everything being black and white or pictures of whiteboards"

"I agree, so lets assume we get hundreds of new outcomes over the next quarter. We know they must be prioritised by the end of week 6 of the quarter. We should use the Three staged Priority Model but we should adapt it slightly.

Three Staged Priority Model

Our first step in the process of any idea or concept, is to understand if it is maintain, continuous improvement or change.

Maintenance of our current products has a higher priority, so if it is helping us maintain the products or services, it goes to the backlog of the team maintaining that product.

If it is a new idea that doesn't change the business but reduces the cost of maintenance, it is continuous improvement. This will go to the second priority, the teams will prioritise these two items themselves, based on their capacity and the impact it will have.

However, if it is changing the business, we need to know if it aligns to the strategic direction. Does it match our WHY, if so which customer is it assigned to, does it fit on the current customer journey? Do we have an objective for it? If we do not, it goes onto the idea bank, as something we are not focussing on this year. Yet, it is kept for future use.

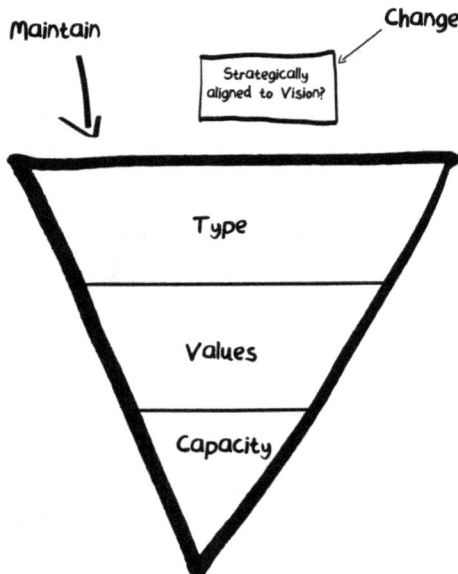

All ideas or concepts that are strategically aligned will need to be prioritised, so again, lets assume we have hundreds that make it through?

We have our metrics that have been set from Rhonda. We are now focussing on sales, loyalty, satisfaction and functional value. "

"Yes but only functional value and sales are the same measurement. They are increased money or decrease costs? Mark was confused how we could map all four together.

"I agree Mark, financial benefits are always the easiest to rank. Firstly we need to weight the metrics. Do we value one over the other? We know Rhonda and Greg have said they are all the same. Which means we don't need to do any complicated weighted average measurements.

We do need to create a range for each, to therefore understand how customer satisfaction is related to sales. That way $4m of cost saving would equal a 15% increase in customer satisfaction. I am sure if we calculated the average long term profit from a customer, then looked at the impact on our bottom line from a 10% increase in customer satisfaction or brand loyalty, we can work it out properly, I think thats something we should look into next year.

For now, I recommend a system of ranking each from one to five. Each idea will need to be measured briefly across each."

"Why over each?"

"Lets say we can reduce costs by ten million but it has an impact of -40% satisfaction and -$1m in revenue?"

"Point taken"

"Then all we need to do is times each score out of five by each and it'll give us a relative number. Something like this" Julie had written a high level table on the whiteboard.

KPI	Very Low	Low	Medium	High	Extreme
Sales per customer	x				
Onboarding cost per customer		x			
Return on Equity		x			
Increase profit against industry inflation			x		
Brand sentiment		x			
Positive feedback				x	
Reduced waste to customer	x				
Higher gross margin			x		

"We need to determine what is 'Very Low for Sales per customer' but once we do we know this is a 1.

In the above example, that would be a score of 15. Its an random number, it means nothing to anyone else but NZFS. If this is the level of customer value we will make from this example outcome. We then need to understand what is the rough cost of the outcome.

We don't want to have to do a lean canvas on every idea, this should merely be a rough time plus materials. It WILL be wrong.

However, it is enough to get us to a value to cost ratio. Which we will be double checking at the lean canvas stage and triple checking at the validation stage.

With all the ideas going into this system, we will be able to plot the ranking by the ratios like this.

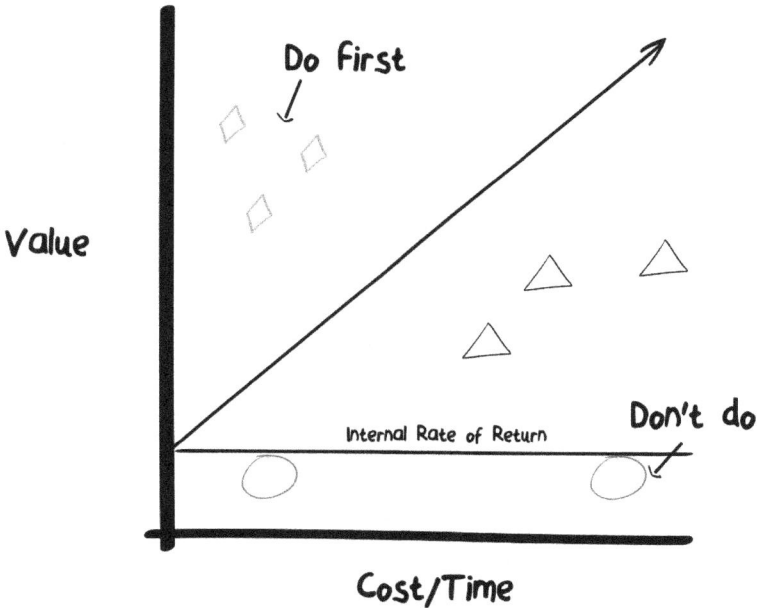

The highest value to cost ratios should be complete first. This will also mean that ideas will get smaller to get larger value to cost ratios.

This will automate the backlog, as long as the most basic analysis is complete up front, we will save a lot of time on product managers having to massage their backlog or making things fit."

"I like a good bit of automation, let me take that action, I'll get the other technology leaders to agree to what is very low to extreme for each and then we can implement this next quarter. Now let's get going, I am sure the teams are super thrilled to start" Mark jumped up and started moving towards the large open space where the developers will be performing the 90 day strategy

Capacity Planning

There wasn't a room large enough to accommodate all 68 people. So Julie had organised to use a level in the building, Whiteboards were put up on wheels everywhere with enough post it notes, pens and string to make any Agile Coach happy.

She didn't have any Agile Coaches. No Scrum Masters, no Agile Leads, in fact Julie was adamant, if you were not delivering the value, you were not involved. The leaders had to sit and watch and if they got involved, would be escorted out. Only Julie was there to facilitate, Harry said she should have been a Agile Coach, she said she preferred the title Agility Consultant. She wasn't coaching anyone, she was running a workshop and helping them achieve the outcome needed.

As Julie walked in there was a lack of energy. People were slumped over chairs and there was a visible sense of groaning in the air. Developers didn't like Agile, they didn't like big room planning, Programme increment (PI) planning or any other false sense of empowerment process.

"Wow don't we all look so happy to be here!" Julie yelled out. Mark was suddenly awake, the calm and methodical Julie had suddenly started bouncing around the room wih energy and..... Shouting.

"I know, I get it, you have been here before. You spend up to two days planning with everyone, only to be told no, then you are told throughout the quarter to change direction and then told how your process should look?

This is not what this is. When we start the new financial year. These outcomes are all we are focusing on. There may be sudden changes, we will adapt, but no one will tell you how to achieve these outcomes. There is no process guides, all I ask is that you reflect weekly on your process. I want you to look at what worked, what didn't work and choose one thing to test the following week.

Everything else is up to you." This made everyone give more attention "It is you, our technology experts who need to tell us, how you will achieve these outcomes, what people you need and also what is possible and not.

As everyone is aware, we have split technology by the work being completed. We believe we have everyone we need in this room to achieve the outcomes on the board. Its up to you to tell us yes, or no.

This will also not take two days. We have booked four hours for this workshop. The inputs to this session?

- Prioritised list of outcomes; illustrated on a lean canvas with assumptions and constraints that have been validated and what has yet to be validated
- An evaluation of the hypothesed skills required to achieve the outcome, some of you had input to determine this, however, raise as soon as possible if this is incorrect
- You have brought your capacity for the coming quarter"

A beaded developer called ray spoke up "What if we didn't understand the capacity homework?"

There was a lot of agreement in the room. Julie pivoted, "Then we shall do it now before we start. You all have your current teams that you work in. I want you to split into those teams, write your team name on a whiteboard and draw a big circle"

The teams started moving into their areas and almost all of the teams wrote their functions as a team name. How boring Julie thought. Apart from the avengers and Justice League, who were competing digital teams, Julie hoped they would dress up one day as well!

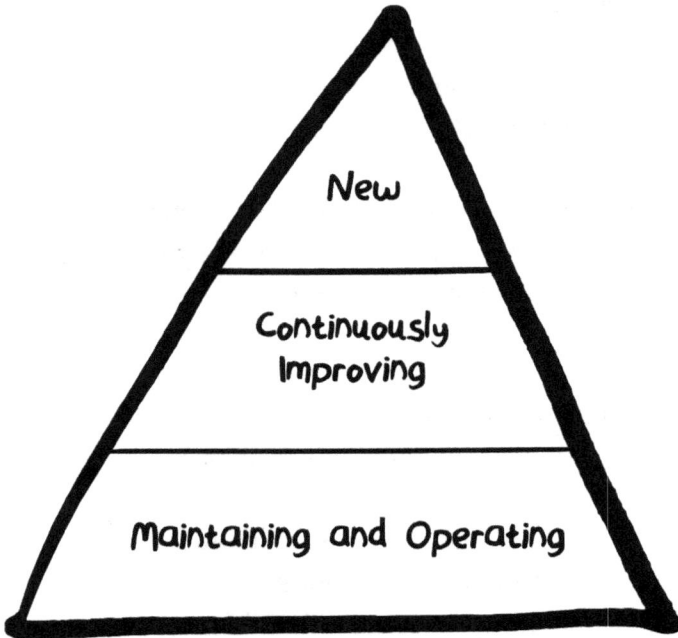

"I want you to think about the last three months. Open up your workflow tools if you need, have a look at how many hours your team spent on maintaining current products or services. How many meetings, how many events and anything that was deemed as business as usual. Take the average over three months.

Then ask your team members, who is having a holiday? Any planned sick leave? How many working days are there in this quarter? Look at the maintenance work to be done and then divide that into the total hours to give a percentage. Shade that part of the circle, Mark will create an average up here for all to see"

This was obviously the first time the teams had ever been asked such a question. Laptops were out, calendars were open and planned sick leave became a running commentary.

The average came back within fifteen minutes, some teams had very low maintain percentages and some were almost 100% maintain. The average was 70%. This meant that if there was no change, 70% of the teams time is just maintaining current systems, processes and products.

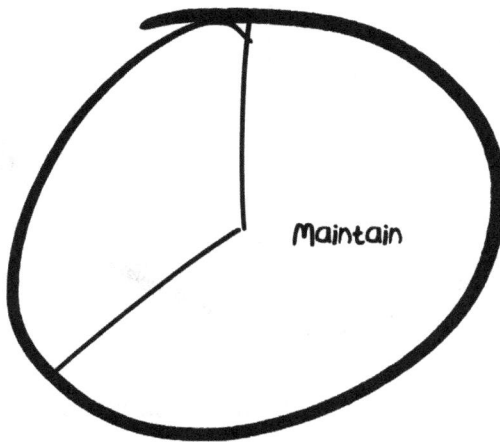

"Who was shocked by that figure" Julie paused and let the number sink in to everyone around the room.

"I have completed this exercise a number of times and I always see a very high number. We forget the level of effort there is in maintaining our current and yet we focus so heavily on frameworks that deliver change. So my next step is to add to that. I want you to add 10% to your workload and call it continuous improvement.

The idea behind continuous improvement is to prioritise process change, technology changes or refactor pre-existing code to be better. If you invest 10% of your time in reducing the amount of maintenance you have to do, it'll leave more time for fun new and challenging items.

For the teams that are 100% maintenance, I want you to talk to your managers about borrowing another person for this quarter, so you can open your capacity up.

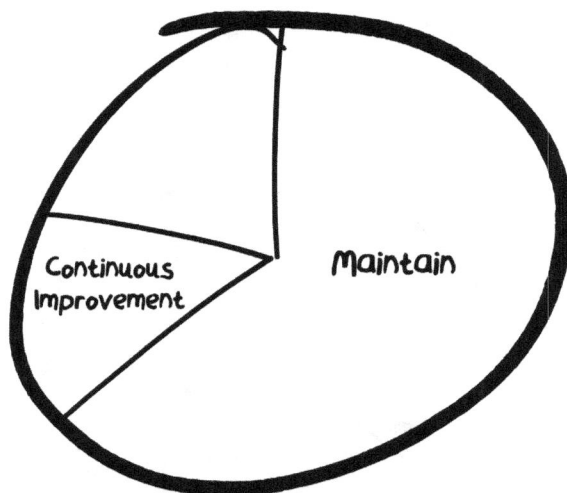

The idea behind today is to fill that circle up to 100% and then stop. Once you have hit 100%, you can commit to those items and head off for an early lunch."

This got the teams excited, most teams only had to fill up 20-30% of their workload. As maintenance can not be planned, it just happens and this was not a continuous improvement workshop, which the teams will need to do as a team. This was just a change planning. How much change can we complete in 90 days.

"Outputs from today will be a list of outputs to deliver as a team, dependencies between teams, timing/sizes of each output, commitment that you can complete the outputs and most importantly, together you can achieve the outcome.

Story Mapping

Up first is Outcome 1: Customers can apply for a mortgage online with everything the mortgage advisers need to complete their application process. You all can see the lean canvas, it has many features assigned to it and is quite complex, hitting a number of systems and processes. "

It was ray who stood up again. "Yes, a number of us looked at that outcome this morning. It can not be complete in a quarter. Its too big, there are far too many features and we have as you can see, very limited capacity. "

Ray wasn't wrong. With 20% overall capacity, this 90 day strategy looks doomed from the start. Julie thought about cancelling, but pushed that thought out of her head quickly! "Lets fill up our capacity first Ray, you never know what you may find?"

Ray seemed to have the most experience on this process. He started working with the other teams to break down the outcome into outputs. Which the teams were calling epics. Weirdly 60 people working on one outcome wasn't as much of a disaster as Julie thought, they all knew their skills and came up with multiple solutions.

Over an hour had gone by with nothing on the boards in terms of outputs. Four teams had decided that they had no input into that outcome and had grabbed the next outcome from the list to break down. Ray called Julie over at the 90 minute Mark.

"Well, we have isolated our options for you down to two." The other leaders were suddenly very close and Julie looked at them sternly, not to outrank the teams, "When we first mapped out this outcome into outputs, we noticed it was eight months work based on our current capacity model. However, we noticed that we were assuming we had to use our legacy systems. We could create a workaround using the new module based system and it can be complete in two."

"Is there any loss of functionality to the customer, do we break any security or compliance issues? Why such a dramatic reduction in time?"

"It is like building a new house vs renovating an old one. Unless you like the character of the old house, sometimes its easier to scrap it and start again. We have so much legacy code that a lot of us do not entirely know how it works. We can however, create a new process and system for capturing online requests instead" Ray responded

"Sounds good to me, your the experts, not me." Ray was surprised by Julies response, he even looked to Harry for confirmation, Harry nodded, the developers were off to the races. Breaking the outcome into weekly chunks of delivery, matching dependencies within the outcome group and outside.

Julie, Mark, Harry and Alex mapped out the return on investment of the original solution vs the new one. Scrapping the functionality required on the legacy system and process, removed negative return on investment. So now we have a better solution, being delivered sooner and at a lower price!

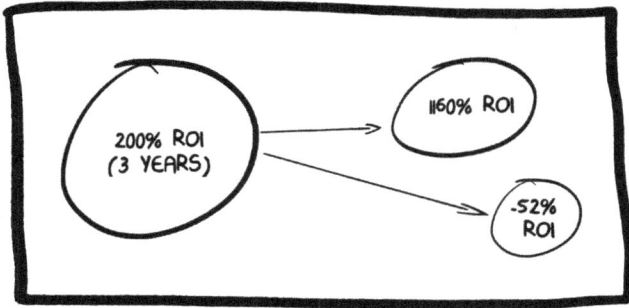

The teams had outputs which were roughly guided by effort, risk and complexity. Some teams were using fibonacci to understand relative size to other pieces of work they knew, some used rocket ships, which Julie did not understand and others were using T-Shirt sizing.

Relative sizing is a technique used for complex deliverables. Where you estimate in an abstract form, instead of hours because you know you are going to be incorrect, but at least you are relatively incorrect together.

The teams only had an hour left, they started breaking the outputs (which were Epics in their workflow system) into stories. There wasn't the time for acceptance test driven development (ATDD), the idea was to have enough detail to estimate time for the stories. ATDD is a model where you use behavioural acceptance criteria like GIVEN an historical event as happen, WHEN a trigger happens, THEN I expect this behaviour.

This acceptance criteria tells the team what success looks like from an experience point of view for the story, then this leads to positive and negative test cases, which tell those who are doing the code development how someone will test it, therefore how to ensure it meets the test cases.

Julie really likes ATDD as the customer drives the user, which drives the testing and finally ends up with less risk, less bugs and more value.

Today wasn't the day to introduce this, today was about getting the stories estimated to fill capacity.

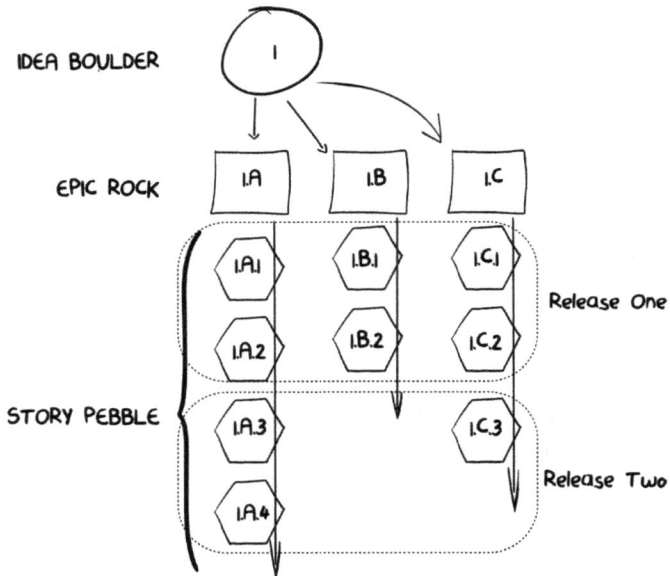

It was ten minutes untill the four hour time slot would ellapse when Julie stood back up to talk to everyone. All nine teams had finished their capacity planning, broken two outcomes into a list of team-based outputs, re-designed solutions to create a list of stories. All stories were estimated in the number of days to complete them and some teams had already broken down their stories into tasks for the first week sprint.

"I want to see how commitment we are to this strategy. When I say, you are going to raise your hand with a number between one and five. If you are super confident in delivering the change, while continuously improving and maintaining your current products and services, you say a five. If you are extremely not confident, you raise a one. Let's see those hands?"

Everyones hand went up, it was mostly fours with the odd three and five. A success by any account. Julie decided not to probe the threes but to note the teams that had them.

"Great news everyone, you have just completed your first 90 day strategy session. You have given commitment. We have two new outcomes our customers can look forward to, you have ring fenced enough time to ensure we keep delivering work and you also have set aside time for continuously improving.

Ways of Working

In What Way you deliver this value, is in your court. I want you to think about what your process is, from the technology leader-ship point of view, we have asked for you to maintain, continuously improve and deliver these outcomes. You have agreed. However, I want you to document the process in which you will do this, then keep updating it each week with improvements. Thank you all for coming, its been a fun four hours."

The teams chose a lot of their process during the session, the other sessions went in a similar way. Most teams wanted to reduce dependencies, therefore created output based teams. Majority of the teams moved to one week sprints, instead of their standard two week, with a weekly start meeting and reflection at the end.

Each team seemed to naturally have a lead, the leads agreed to meet weekly as well to manage any dependencies and lastly, they wanted to show their outputs working to each other at 4pm on a Friday over work drinks. Julie may have influenced a bit with the task sizing, but everyone seemed happy that the start of the week will have a list of tasks for the week and each member would just complete one per day, making the number easier to predict.

Teams also liked the idea that once an outcome was complete, they would be the ones maintaining it. On the AcDC it would go into the maintenance column, it would increase their maintenance cost, which hopefully the continuous improvement would offset.

If an outcome fails its assumption, validation or during development new information was found, it would go straight to the Dead column. Lessons learnt would be found, so that we didn't complete the same mistake again.

The other sessions went well, the workflow tool was filled up with 4 objectives, 29 potential outcomes, 7 outcomes will start in two weeks time with commitment for 5 of them to be completed by the end of the quarter.

"If we get this complete Julie, we would be making a dramatic impact on our customer needs" Said Harry

The technology leadership were having end of week work drink and everyone seemed rather happy with themselves.

"I agree, this will be the first time NZFS has delivered any capital projects in under 90 days. Finance has already agreed to the funding drawdown. Since we didn't ask for any new people, I don't see how they could say no. We have showed them the lean canvases, the process, the resources and the KPIs we are looking to hit." Alex didn't smile often but with a glass of red in his hand, he couldn't stop.

Mark took a sip of his whisky, "our amazing teams have showed us what they can do, all we needed to do was support them, provide the required vision and get out of the way.

On our workflow management tool, you can clearly see the percentage complete of each objective, we know rough sizes of the outcomes, allowing us to plan into the future and the teams hopefully will create the process they need in order to be high performing!"

"It has been a very good week team. I like your point Mark, we need to be able to plan past the quarter for people needs, infra-structure projects, projects the PMO might throw at us and for the board. Why don't we set up a dynamic roadmap next week?"

Week 11
Dynamic Roadmaps

Tuesday mornings became Julies favourite moment in the week, most people seem to be in the office and the whole place buzzes with excitement. As oppose to Monday and Fridays, which seem to be everyone's work from home day, including the contractors who were able to negotiate their ability to work from home as well. Julie and the other technology leaders agreed that there is no difference between the contractors and the permanent staff, they are all delivering value and should have the same benefits.

"So what is the difference between a gantt chart, a roadmap and a dynamic roadmap Julie" Mark was looking a little worried, he sat down with his long black

"The reason I ask, we spend a long time fighting against the project managers and their gantt charts. These fictional timelines for when we will be complete and yet all gantt charts do, is show us a moment in time. Then we went agile and the project managers created roadmaps.

The roadmaps looked exactly the same as project gantt charts, except they had a fresh look, were focused on the product and were agile. So now you are bringing dynamic roadmaps. Which again just look like a gantt chart but more people are involved? I just don't get it."

"Fair point Mark" Julie closed the document she was reading and gave Mark her full attention. "As leaders we focus on the vision and the objectives but we are also accountable for supporting the staff to ensure they are able to deliver the best work they can, correct?"

Mark nodded

"As leaders we are looking down on the dance floor, we are not the ones actually dancing, we are too far away to see the detail and therefore we shouldn't tell people how to dance. We do however, have a responsibility to ensure people don't fall off a cliff, fall over and that we have the right amount of dancers to achieve the event we all set out for.

So as leaders, we need a high level map of where we are at, at any given time. I agree that gantt charts are too rigid and are normally controlled by one person trying to gather information. Roadmaps are exactly the same but we replace Project Managers with Product Owners.

What I am talking about is an automated system. A view of the world that ensures we can see and plan six months, a year out. Data driven decision making, data that gets more accurate the closer we get to delivery."

"So how do we automate the gantt chart, I mean dynamic roadmap?" Mark said

"You have been working with the KPI matrix. So we are going to be able to prioritise the outcomes automatically from the start of the year, which means anyone that adds an outcome into the backlog, it'll automatically prioritise. We should do this with Microsoft forms and sharePoint.

With sharePoint we can create a page explaining the process and showing the current outcomes in order per objective.

With forms, we can ask the right questions that allow the idea or concept to get placed onto the backlog. Firstly we use power automate to trigger if this outcome is strategically aligned to one of the outcomes, if it isn't, it needs to go into the "idea bank" and an email is sent to the requestor automatically.

If it is aligned to the objective, the objective owner will need to get some rough costs. This will give the full prioritisation and the requestor will get an email of its number in the queue AND a rough date of start."

"How will we know when we can work on it???" Mark was shocked by this

"That is the purpose behind a dynamic roadmap. It is assumption and data driven, as the assumptions get clearer, the time lines get more accurate.

Here is the stages each go through." Julie drew the idea to delivery process on a near by whiteboard.

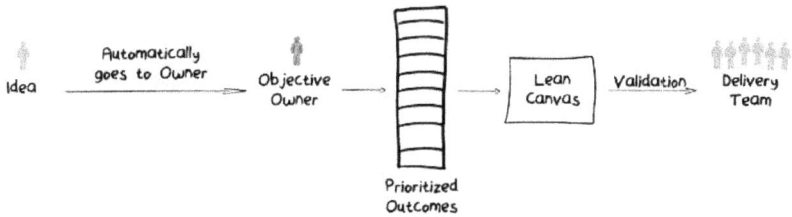

Idea — Automatically goes to Owner → Objective Owner → [Prioritized Outcomes] → Lean Canvas — Validation → Delivery Team

"Now as you can see, if we automate the outcomes going into the backlog, an objective owner can add some costs, then we will know as outcomes are delivered, more are going into validation, which is pulling more into lean canvas and shifting the prioritisation.

As long as we are transparent that the priority is set by the value to cost ratios. It'll limit the push back from our internal stakeholders.

So now we have ideas being raised and placed into the outcome backlog via SharePoint, forms, and power automate (which is a Microsoft automation tool that uses events to do an action for us) for communications. We just need to follow the timelines of lean canvas, validation and delivery. Measuring the time it takes the average outcome to get to delivery and the accuracy of commitment to complete vs the actual completion of the outcome. "

"Ah so if an outcome was meant to take sixty days and it actually takes ninety, this will push back the other outcomes and create a variance for future outcomes?" Mark clicked how the dynamics would work.

"Yes, absolutely, so for instance, I am pulling in the workflow tool data into power BI now. I can see that our four objectives are 0% complete and we anticipate objective one to be 100% complete by the end of quarter three. I can choose an outcome and see the outputs and there timelines and which teams are associated with the outputs.

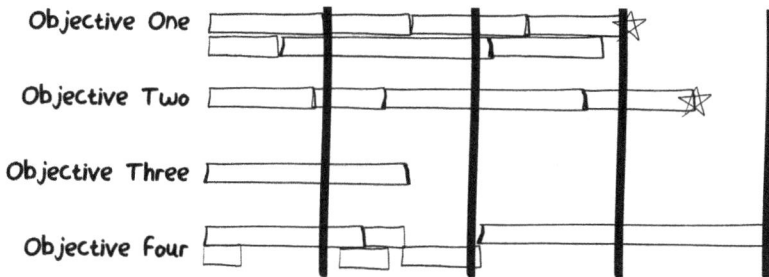

So I now have a bird's eye view of all technology work, every day I open it, the developers task data will update the anticipated output completion date, the outputs will then give me an update on outcomes and this will shift the start date of the next outcome, because we have a fixed number of people.

If the outcomes slip, we can see the impact further down the line and best of all if the planned time and actual times creates a variance, we can automatically put a buffer in. Lastly, if new ideas that are better then what we have, come into the backlog, the dynamic roadmap will update with those ideas! "

"Ok, this is actually really good, so we won't be delivering this as a report to the board every quarter, you will have it as a living document in SharePoint and Power BI?" said Mark

"Absolutely! The requestor and the stakeholders will automatically get updates on their ideas, the teams know what is to come and we are continuously adapting the roadmap based on customer data, internal stakeholder data and lastly, delivery data."

"I can actually see a problem now." Mark was looking at objective three and four

"What do you see Mark?"

"Well objective three and four will not be completed in time but more important than that, objective three loses a lot of contractors after quarter two, in September we have an audit as well, so thats why capacity has decreased. Great, this is telling us before quarter one, that we will have problems in September with the number of people we need to keep the outcomes flowing!"

"Good point, I hadn't realised there was a timing issue with the audit, no wonder capacity decreases in that period. So now we know we either need more people or reduce our expectations on objective four?

Great news, we have six months to resolve that issue! We also haven't factored in continuous improvement. As the teams build their processes and iterate them, we should see more capacity each quarter for change. Meaning we will increase throughput.

We need to enter in the number of people and their skill sets into our database as well. This will mean we can raise automatically if an outcome requires a skill that the objective band does not have OR there becomes a constraint on that skill that means training or hiring is needed.

I am really interested to see what metrics they use, I will be managing lead time. Thats the time from when someone raises an idea to the time it is completed and cycle time, which is the time the work begins and is finished.

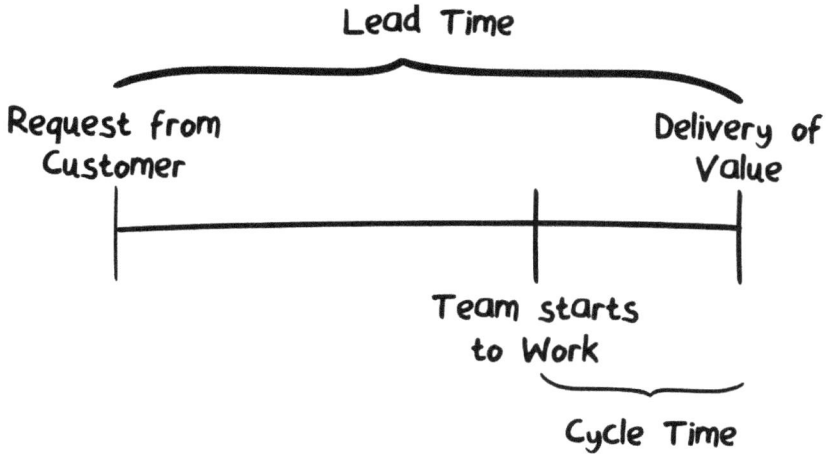

Lead Time

Request from Customer — Delivery of Value

Team starts to Work

Cycle Time

"Something we also need to introduce at some point would be what the teams on objective one found. How valuable is each feature inside the outcome. We know the industry likes Must Haves, Should Haves, Could Haves and Won't have (MoSCoW).

It would be great to have this mapped out in terms of value. Each feature or element of an outcome mapped against effort. We could do this in the validation phase?" Julie was on a roll.

"It would make sense to do in the validation phase, that way the teams only pull in the most valuable parts of the outcome, ensuring the outcome success criteria is met but the waste isn't brought into the delivery system." Mark drew up the idea of value being delivered would slowly decrease over the length of the outcome, yet the time would be static.

"This means that as the value flattens off for one output, they would move onto the next, ensuring only the appropriate value to time ratios were delivered, reducing waste in the delivery process, BEFORE we start. I like it."

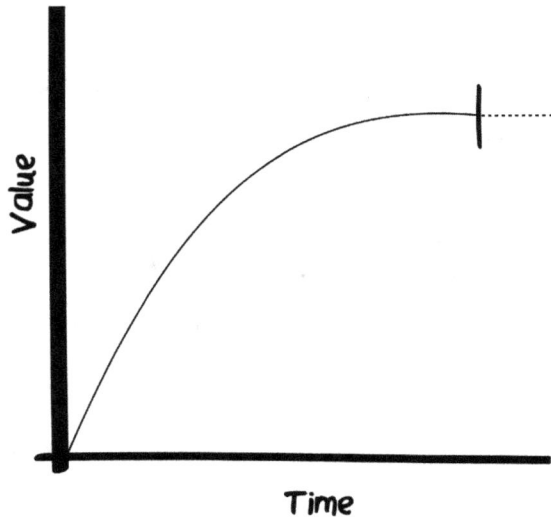

"Its been a fun 10 weeks hasn't it Mark. I do not know if you have noticed, I have put a reflection meeting in your calendar for next week. Just you and me, to talk about what we have done these last three months and what changes we would like to move forward with."

"Yes I have and I'll be there, speaking of changes, have you noticed some of the teams have introduced Scrum, even hiring some ScrumMasters from the PMO, which I suspect is the Project Managers with new titles?"

"No I didn't, but it makes sense. They see this delivery framework as an agile one and a lot of people associate agile with Scrum. Even though we haven't mentioned agile or scrum. Its the teams choice, as long as they are reflecting on their process and keep changing it to benefit the delivery, I see no harm."

Julies phone rings, its Darren

"Good timing Darren, how are things?" Julie had totally forgotten about the project managers until Mark mentioned them

"Things are good Julie, we will delivering and closing off projects for the next month, the PMO have some concerns about the delivery framework and I thought I would just phone you myself. We are being sent on a two day ScrumMaster course to widen our value to the technology delivery." Darren sounded like he had been hit in the gut.

"More knowledge is always a good thing Darren, I would say however, nothing has changed. The projects that stakeholders give you to do, you still will be doing, we are just helping you with automation"

Darren didn't seem convinced, Julie knew this change would feel like we are pushing project managers away.

"Ok lets go through the roles and responsibilities of a Project Manager. At a high level you:
- Identify and manage the stakeholders
- Identify the project goal
- Identify the requirements
- Identify the project deliverables and success criteria
- Develop a project plan
- Create a resource management plan
- Build a project schedule
- Identify risks, dependencies and constraints
- Work with delivery teams and escalate issues to stakeholders

Sound about right?

"Always fun to have your job put into a paragraph, but yes, that is the key areas of focus for my projects."

"Right, so all we have done is given you a fixed capacity for change, so you now know exactly how much capacity the teams have for projects. All projects will go into a master backlog and must be linked to strategic objectives.

The project resources and schedule and a lot of stakeholder management can be automated for you but you will still need to create audit reports on capex projects. You will still need to work with the teams to remove blockers for them and if you want to, you can ask them if you can be their scrum master, which means serving them, helping them improve their flow and reporting up any risks or issues.

Very similar to your role now. I'll send you a teams message to show you the delta between the PMO Project Management process and what I believe is the VMO, the value management office outcome delivery process. "

Darren was silent for a bit, then responded "I actually think you might be right. This gives us more time to do what we are good at, less time on things that we struggle to keep up with."
"Great news Darren, let the PMO know, I am not out to get them and I'll forward you this picture of PMO vs VMO."

Julie didn't have the heart to tell Darren that her teams have already scrapped Scrum. They have the advantage of iterating the past few weeks into a flow that suits them and their outcomes. It doesn't involve Scrum. She sent the PMO vs VMO matrix to make them more comfortable that this wasnt' an attack on project management.

PMO	VMO
Identify and manage the stake-holders	Must still be completed in Lean Canvas, during the validation and during delivery.
Identify the project goal	Must be complete inside the outcome form
Identify the requirements	Must be complete inside the outcome form
Identify the project deliverables and success criteria	Must be complete inside the outcome form
Develop a project plan	Automated via Dynamic Road-map
Create a resource management plan	Automated via Dynamic Road-map for people, however, any external costs will need to be on top
Build a project schedule	Automated via Dynamic Road-maps
Identify risks, dependencies and constraints	Still required from Ideation to Delivery
Work with delivery teams and escalate issues to stakeholders	Still required to escalate but not required to manage

Reflection

Julie enjoyed the rest of her week, as projects were closing there was the fun of work being tossed over to her team and the priority incidents that came with it. Julie knew this wasn't going to last much longer, the new structure started next week and there was already changes being found in the culture of the teams.

It was a calm Monday morning, most people seemed to be working from home and Mark was reading over the email that Julie had sent last week about the importance of Reflection. At least it was short, he thought.

Reflection is the act of taking time to think about and analyze your experiences, thoughts, and feelings. It can be a powerful tool for personal growth and development, as it allows you to better understand yourself and your motivations, as well as identify areas for improvement.

There are several benefits to reflection:

1. Improved self-awareness: Reflection helps you to better understand your strengths, weaknesses, values, and beliefs. This can help you make more informed decisions about your life and career.
2. Enhanced problem-solving skills: By thinking about your experiences, you can identify patterns and insights that can help you solve problems more effectively in the future.
3. Increased creativity: Reflection can help stimulate new ideas and perspectives, leading to increased creativity and innovation.
4. Greater self-regulation: Reflection can help you become more self-aware of your emotions and behaviors, allowing you to better regulate and control them.
5. Enhanced learning: By thinking about what you have learned and how you have grown, you can more effectively retain and apply new information in the future.

To engage in reflection, you can try the following steps:

1. Set aside time: Choose a quiet, comfortable place where you can reflect without distractions.
2. Reflect on your experiences: Think about a specific experience or event that you want to reflect on. Consider what you did, what you thought and felt, and what you learned from the experience.
3. Write it down: Write down your thoughts and feelings about the experience. This can help you better process and understand them.
4. Analyze and interpret: Consider what the experience means to you and how it has affected you. What did you learn about yourself and others? How has the experience changed your perspective or behavior?
5. Take action: Based on your reflections, consider what you

can do differently in the future to improve your experiences or achieve your goals.

6. It's important to make reflection a regular practice, rather than just doing it once in a while. Set aside time each day or week to reflect on your experiences and make it a habit.

"Your email mentions we should do this daily and yet this is our first one?" Mark loved to start off pointing out things.

"Yes Mark, we really should have been reflecting throughout this process, its not until you take a breathe can you really admire what is going on. I apologise, however, we have lots to look at. Shall we start with where we were?"

"Sure, our original BAR showed a lot of issues; hope you don't mind, I named it the Business Agility Radar, or BAR."

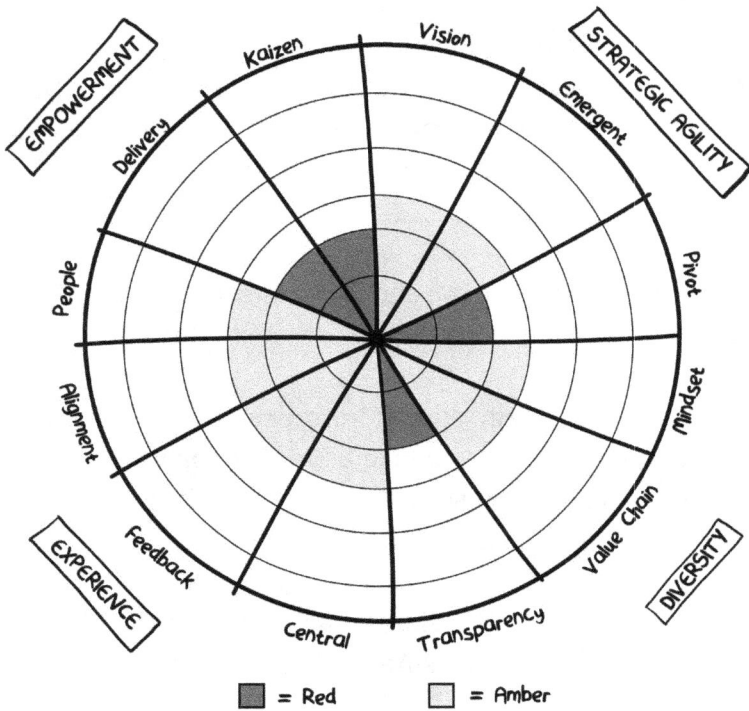

Vision · Emergent · Pivot · Mindset · Value Chain · Transparency · Central · Feedback · Alignment · People · Delivery · Kaizen

STRATEGIC AGILITY · DIVERSITY · EXPERIENCE · EMPOWERMENT

■ = Red   □ = Amber

"I agree, four red areas, causing a lot of the issues we were having regularly. Then we had a separation between developing new solutions and maintaining them, our framework wasn't really set up for successful delivery in a complex world."

"Don't forget our KPIs, they were measuring how well we delivered outputs. Not how much value we delivered to the customer. So we didn't know what benefits we were getting or not getting for years."

"True, although we can not take credit, we influenced those KPIs nicely. So lets re assess our BAR:

Strategic Agility

Vision - *One Strategic Vision for all to see and work towards* - Our new framework doesn't impact the leadership styles, so we are **Amber** here.

Emergent - *30-120 day strategy plans are being used with a single prioritised backlog* - our new delivery framework moves us into **Orange**, to focus on delivering outcomes quarterly

Pivot - *Lean business canvas or similar are produced and approved within a financial quarter, with either a focus on competition or value metric* - We introduced the AcDC which focused on the lean business cavas and financial drawdown on outcomes quarterly. **Orange**.

Cognitive Diversity

Mindset - *Prescribed feedback is given to individuals and training courses are booked* - no move here, this is a leadership and HR change we would need to make. **Amber**

Value chain - *Teams work within functional silos within single value chain and/or no customer has been engaged* - Having teams work at an objective level, we move to **Orange**. Still functional silos however.

Transparency - *Organisation knowledge is communicated and stored centrally* - Data and documents are now available online, however, its still behind authority walls. **Amber**

Customer Experience

Customer at the centre - *Personas are created by Design teams outside our Tribe* - I do not think we fully understand the customer, we moved to the framework that allows us to really understand the customer, but it was us leaders who did the customer journey maps. **Amber**

Customer Feedback - *Feedback is requested after delivery of value* - Although we have a framework that can engage and get customer feedback, we are still requesting it after the quarter. **Amber**

Customer Alignment - *Centralised vision for customer value but implemented by individuals differently* - We now have customer value KPIs. **Orange**

Employee Empowerment

People - *Autonomous teams have been created with individual KPIs and management lines and/or team members have titles with individual responsibilities* - Our delivery framework allows us to create work to the people, not people to the work. **Orange**

Agile Delivery - *Organisation have implemented a framework such as SAFe or DA to ensure whole value chains are included in iterative delivery* - We moved to **Orange** here with our framework.

Kaizen - *A leader measures outcomes to see if improvements can be made - such as Six Sigma* - Our technology leadership team has now taken control of our continuous improvement process. **Orange** "

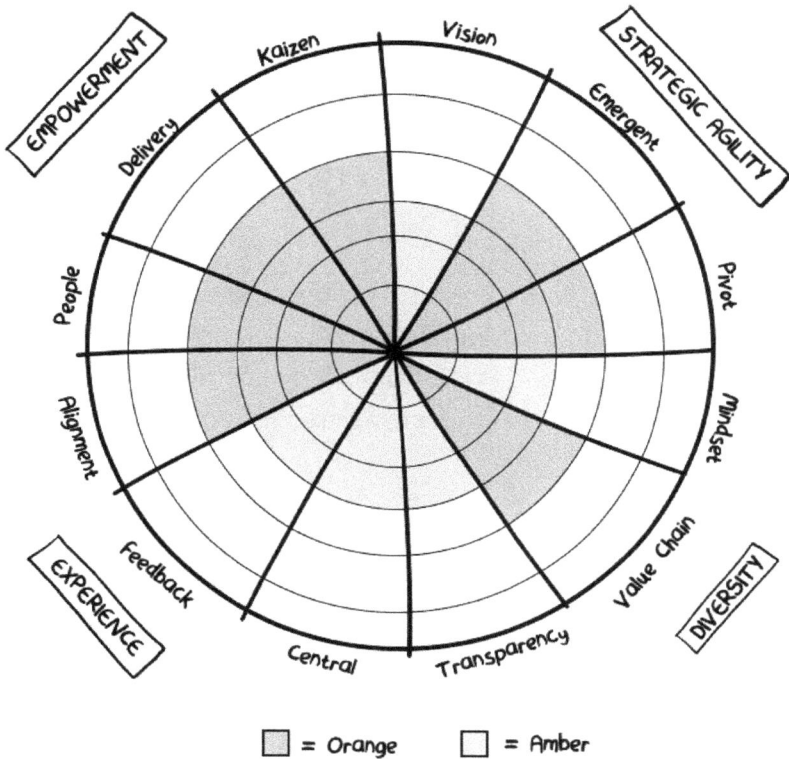

EMPOWERMENT
STRATEGIC AGILITY
EXPERIENCE
DIVERSITY

Kaizen
Vision
Emergent
Delivery
Pivot
People
Mindset
Alignment
Value Chain
Feedback
Transparency
Central

☐ = Orange   ☐ = Amber

"Wow Julie, we went from four reds and the rest Amber, showing that we were solely focused on efficiency with some authoritarian leadership practices, to mostly Orange, which is outcome and productivity focused. That suits NZFS more, I would think" Mark looked thrilled.

"We will let the data decide Mark, we should see our leading KPIs move over the next twelve months and that should flow through into our lagging profit indicators."

"I guess the reflection would be to focus the next twelve months on leadership practices and how value is moved from one area of the business to the other?" Mark was perplexed on how to do this.

"Agreed, also agree that this will be hard. We made the changes in technology but now we need to understand how to ensure these changes are from end to end of the customer journey."

Mark wrote up on the whiteboard the new **customer value metrics**.

"Now lets not forget a major win, the whole organisation is now looking at leading indicators from your customer value system. Brand Loyalty, Sale and Price, Customer satisfaction and Functional Value. With two KPIs for each, where all work is linked to."

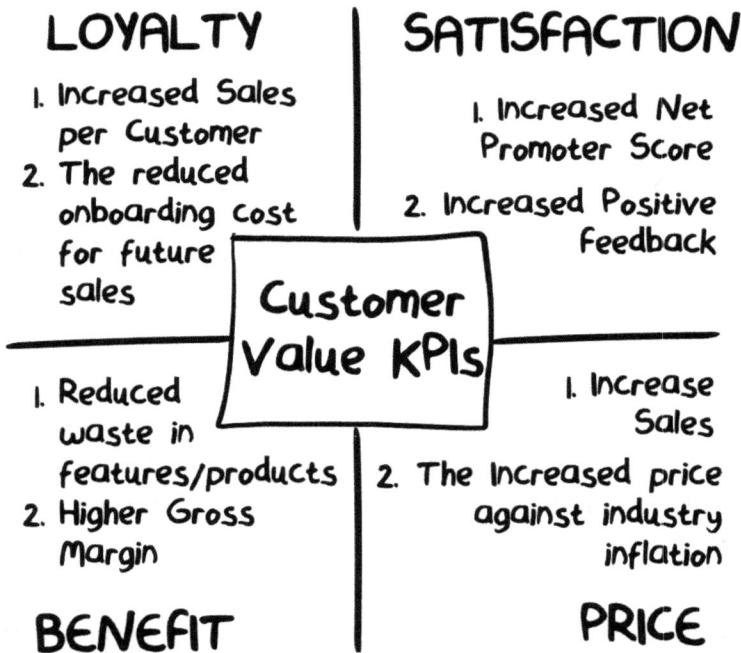

LOYALTY

1. Increased Sales per Customer
2. The reduced onboarding cost for future sales

SATISFACTION

1. Increased Net Promoter Score
2. Increased Positive Feedback

Customer Value KPIs

1. Reduced waste in features/products
2. Higher Gross Margin

1. Increase Sales
2. The Increased price against industry inflation

BENEFIT

PRICE

"Yes that was a surprise. I have only met Rhonda once and she ran with those metrics straight away, even with Greg being negative. We need to make sure these work, my reflection here is to really focus on data driven decision making and ensuring our framework is set up to maximise those KPIs."

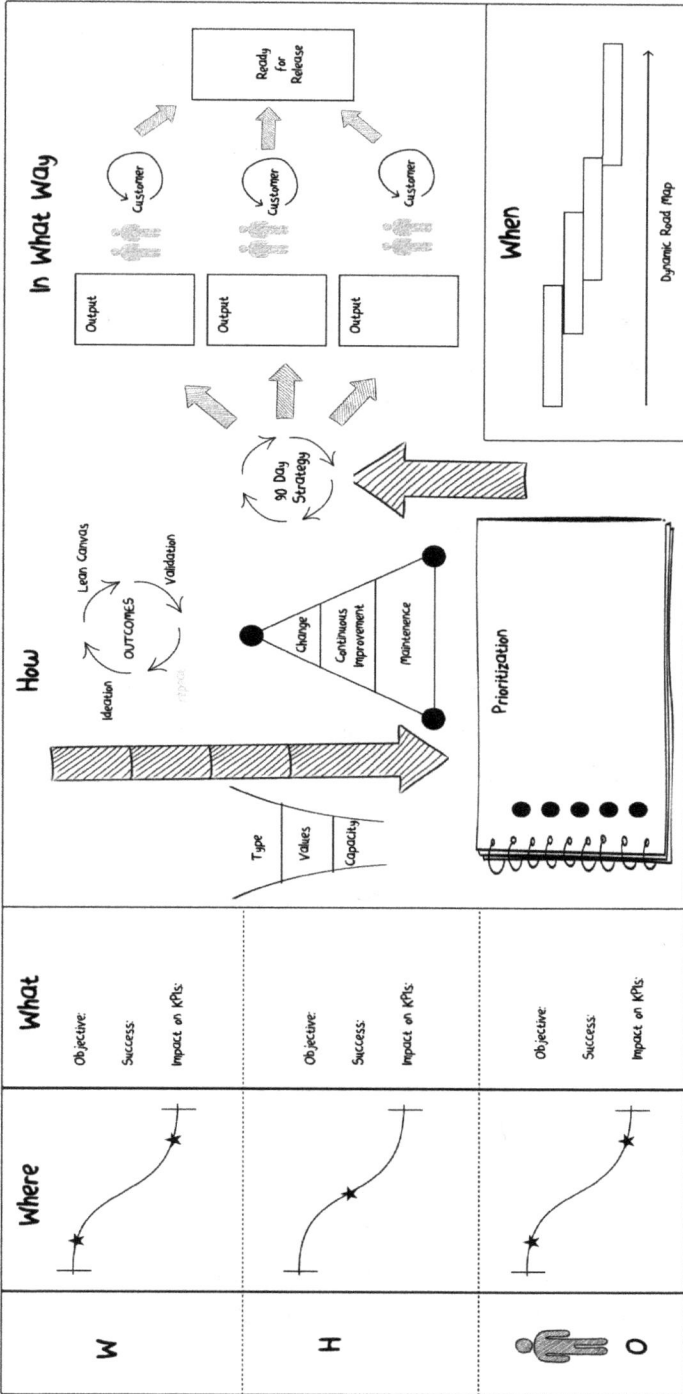

Why + Customer Value KPIs

"Our delivery model has completely changed. I have named this for you Julie. I call it the **ASO framework**. As in Amber Seeking Orange. I think we will need to create a slightly different version for OSG, Orange Seeking Green. We also need to know that if we change something, it is actually increasing customer value, otherwise we will be changing for change sake."

"Very true Mark, So we have introduced the **7 Circumstances of Strategy** for helping us with our adaptive strategy. This allowed us to segment our work by one objective per customer.

We used the **Agile Delivery Canvas (AcDC)** to visualise on a page how we are testing hypothesis to achieve an objective for the customer.

We have automated the prioritisation of the outcomes, that our internal stakeholders believe will help us achieve the objectives. A simple zero to five ranking for each KPI using the **three staged priority model.**"

Mark interrupted "Don't forget the Maintain, Continuous Improvement and Change segmentation of the employees. This was massive Julie, for the first time, we actually understood the cost to maintain our business, we keep driving down that cost with continuous improvements and now have a set amount of time for change."

"Yes and that change all starts with the **90 day strategy** workshop. Ensuring those that are closest to the work, break an outcome down into the outputs, they will deliver. This gave us commitment and meant the teams would create their own process to deliver the outputs in the best way.

This diagram allows us to show how the organisation works, with its Why: mission statement, Who: our value chains, Where: our customer journey maps, What: our objectives for the year and then our How, In What Way and When is a dynamic system which is both bottom up and top down.

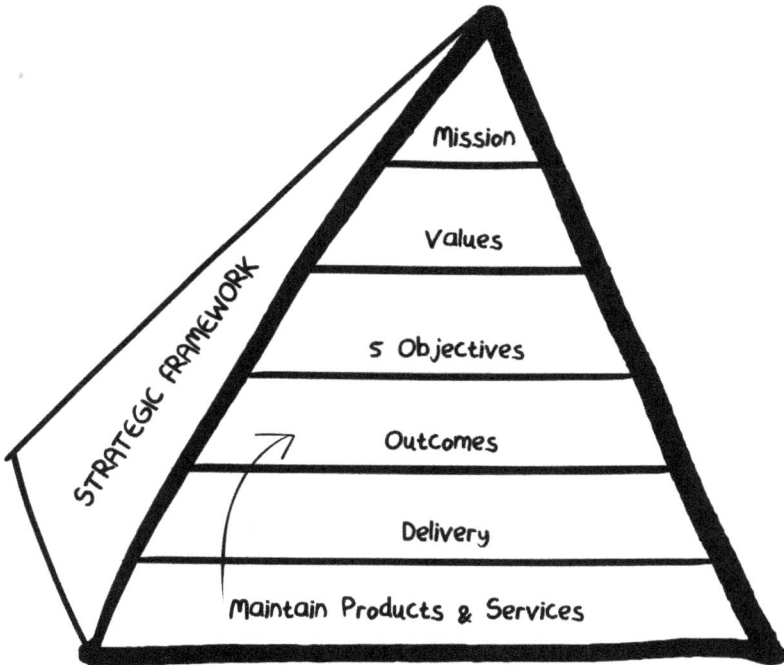

Lastly, we now have a fully automated **dynamic roadmap**, its online, everyone can see it and it updates with the work being completed today, for outcomes months from now. Mix that in with benefit realisation and we can map and track cost to benefit ratios moving forward.

I like your name, the ASO delivery framework. It meets the teams and NZFS where they are now, while allowing flexibility to move to orange. You are right, more customer involvement will be needed to move to green. Which will mean this framework will be tweaked."

"Thank you Julie. When I first spoke to you, I thought you could help me achieve my vision, I realise now, I was trying to change the world and not making the first step easy.

Working with you, I can see, if we break things into small incremental steps, we can dramatically change where we end up, instead of what I did. Complain for five years. " Mark was upset and happy at the same time, a strange mix.

"Mark, you paved the way, If you hadn't laid the ground work, the small steps wouldn't have happened. We are each others champions. Now the idea is to ensure we find more champions and then ask them to find more, so we compound the changes across the organisation.

I have my three month meeting with Greg now. So we shall find out if I have a job next week. Remember, in New Zealand you can be fired within the first three months for no reason!"

Julie laughed, she knew it was highly unlikely, but he technically could...

"One last question Julie? I know we only loosely followed reinventing organisation but what happens to Teal? A lot of people around the world talk about Teal?"

Julie stood up and starting walking while laughing to herself.

"Teal doesn't exist. Talk soon Mark"

~

As Julie made her way up to level 28, she was extremely happy with what she had achieved with her champion Mark and her amazing team. Nothing Greg could say, could take away from the fact that her team had improved their employee engagement from 10% to 80%, that their productivity had improved by 178%, predictability of timelines increased by 92%, internal satisfaction is up 15% and time to market reduced on average from 90 days to just 14.

These results are something any General Manager of Technology would love to have.

Julie opened the door and was surprised to see Greg and Rhonda sitting there.

"Julie welcome. I brought Rhonda along to talk about the proposals as it has a wider impact than just technology." Greg went straight to business as usual, Julie suspected it was Rhonda who asked to be here by the tone of Greg's voice.

"I would like to make some changes in the structure of our delivery model. At the moment your teams are focused on multiple areas of the business, we are siloed by the functional division and the new framework I approved with the customer value metrics that Rhonda developed, leans us to focus delivery across the value chains instead."

Rhonda cut Greg off, "Hi Julie, Greg is correct, the new delivery model and customer value KPIs has made the executive team re think how we deliver work at NZFS. We want to be more involved with the customer, respond faster to their changes and not be strict with any of our processes.

I believe Mark gave me a number of your presentation decks, I like this term Agility. I want NZFS to adapt to respond to customer needs, in a flexible way. I want to be agnostic of how we do that and I believe what Greg is proposing is a good first step."

Greg put his serious voice on, that voice you do when you realise your under pressure to perform. It is interesting how this nice women can make Greg be more professional.

"Congratulations, you have a promotion. We have looked at the retail and digital and cards value chain. Harry is leaving us at the end of the month, he has taken a job with another financial entity and we wish him well.

This gives us an opportunity to restructure the technology leadership team. I want to combine your team, the digital team and a few others, so that we can deliver all technology requirements for digital and cards with no dependencies outside of the business unit."

Julie felt like this was a trick, I believe they call it a glass cliff, where you are provided more responsibility, yet set up to fail. Then everyone says look, Julie failed, it obviously can not be done.

Julie took a deep breathe and thought about her words very carefully.

"Thank you both for this recognition. It has been a hard three months and the teams have done amazingly well. What I would ask, if what you want is agility. If you want to adapt this organisation to respond to the customer needs, in a flexible way?

I need the whole value chain. I recommend a pilot, which I would run. Everyone from finance, HR, operations and technology who give value to the digital and cards space, should be in one group, I like to call it a tribe. I believe its 67% technology already and around 257 people.

I do not need a fancy title. I would merely be the customer owner. We would serve Brad the niche customer segmentation in full.

With any products and services that maximise the value to Brad and maximises the return from that Market.

It would be as if we were a separate company, within NZFS.

This would be a true pilot, it would allow the changes that we have already met to go against the next horizon of changes in a pilot. Digital and cards isn't our number one earner, so there is less risk to this experiment, but it will give you the data you need to know if this is a worth while transformation."

There was silence for almost a minute. Rhonda and Greg caught looks until finally Greg took the opportunity.

"I do not think this is something we can agree to here, lets give it twelve months as just technology until we start bringing in everyone else Julie."

"I disagree." Said Rhonda. "If we just have technology involved, it would cause barriers throughout the organisation. The way that Julie is proposing, would allow us to fully test an integrated model around a customer. I like it. Any other conditions Julie?"

"We change the WAR Room name to the Alliance room." Julie said quickly, as if it had been on her mind for months.

"Done. I look forward to working with our first Customer Owner of Digital and Cards. Thank you Julie."

Julie picked up her kids from school on the way home. It might have been the first time she had done this in the three months of NZFS.

While enjoying a Kapiti ice cream with the kids, Julie had a moment of clarity. She had decided this was going to be the outcome, before she joined NZFS.

She focused on the current state, a vision for the future and took advantage of each pain point to complete an incremental step in the right direction. Her champion Mark was invaluable and although this may be a monumentous occasion, Julie was fully aware, this was merely part one. Horizon one. Stage one. Of her three stage journey. It didn't mean she could not enjoy the moment.

Conclusion

For medium to large companies, agility isn't a choice. How far you go with your transformation is not up to you. It is up to the employees and the customers. It is people-driven, people led and measured by people.

Julie joined a company much like your own, sitting clearly in amber, set up for efficiency and short-term profits, one that would have a high competitive advantage in the 1920s. Like NZFS, your company could be at risk of losing Market share to companies faster at responding to customer needs.

Your board of directors may be focused heavily on return on investment, return on equity or Market share against other incumbent companies. Yet we see more and more new companies emerge from what seems thin air; the barriers to entry that were once there have vanished. Competitive advantage will continue to decrease for incumbents afraid of change.

Investing in moving your organisation one step at a time towards greater agility is a must-have. How far you go will be measured by the data. Keep pushing the boundaries until the cost of change exceeds the rewards.

I have given you a few tools on your tool belt in this book. They are agnostic of fads and based on empirical evidence. You need to know where you are now and where you are going, have measurements of success that tell you it's the right path, and lastly, you need a strategic roadmap that adapts to the changes that WILL happen. People are complex; you need to be ready for changes in your organisation and your plan.

Where to now?

This book scratched the surface of agility, adaptive strategy, design thinking, agile delivery, organisational structure and lean. It was designed to answer four specific questions and give potential solutions to the initial stages of a transformation.

You may have noticed that Julie's story still needs to be completed. Julie has her champions and now the authority to lead a value chain as the customer-owner. In the next book in the series, we will look at the next twelve months of Julie's journey, looking at how high performance is derived through the end-to-end value structures of an organisation and leadership techniques. Julie will set up a pilot to show the value of agility when not constrained to a functional silo. Lastly, the final book in the series will follow Julie over the multi-year organisational transformation for NZFS.

If you want to learn more about your organisation, head to www.AgilityMatters.nz, where we have placed more info on all of the tools in this book, and my entire Business Agility Foundations course can be found for free.

**"Unless someone like you cares a whole awful lot,
Nothing is going to get better. It's not."**

- Dr Seuss

Biography

Cr Michael Law eMBA,
Has been working in business development for 20 years and working with New Zealand and Australian transformations for 10; across the banking and public sector.

He has an executive masters of business administration from Massey University, is a qualified scrum master and a global trainer for business agility through ICAGILE.

Currently the Chief Vision Officer (CVO) for Surge Consulting (www. SurgeConsulting.co.nz), a management consultancy that partners with leaders to increase customer value, the CVO for Necta (www. Necta.nz), a machine learning and AI technology company that simplifies the end to end talent acquisition and management of people, and a Councillor for the Whanganui District in New Zealand.

References

1   Millar, C. C. J. M., Groth, O., & Mahon, J. F. (2018). Management InCalifornia Management Review, 61(1), 5–14.

2   Arons, M., Driest, F., & Weed, K. (2014). The Ultimate Marketing Machine. Harvard Business Review, July-August 2014.

3   Pearce, J. A., Freeman, E. B., & Robinson, R. B. (1987). The Tenuous Link between Formal Strategic Planning and Financial Performance.

4   George, B., Walker, R. M., & Monster, J. (2019). Does Strategic Planning Improve Organisational Performance? A Meta-Analysis. Public Administration Review

5   Zahid Yousaf, & Abdul Majid. (2018). Organisational network and strategic business performance : Does organisational flexibility and entrepreneurial orientation really matter?

6   Weber Y, Tarba SY. Strategic Agility: A State of the Art.

7   Kane, Gerald C., Doug Palmer, Anh Nguyen Phillips, David Kiron, and Natasha Buckley (2016), "Aligning the Organisation for Its Digital Future,"

8   Morton, Stacey and Mohn, Building and Maintaining Strategic Agility: An Agenda and Framework for Executive IT leaders

9   Gelhard, C., & Von Delft, S. (2016). The role of organisational capabilities in achieving superior sustainability performance.

10 Zahra, Shaker A., Harry J. Sapienza, and Per Davidsson (2006), "Entrepreneurship and Dynamic Capabilities: A Review, Model and Research Agenda*," Journal of Management Studies, 43 (4),

11 Teece, David J., Gary Pisano, and Amy Shuen (1997), "Dynamic Capabilities and Strategic Management," Strategic Management Journal, 18 (7), 509-33

12 Lee, J.-Y., & Day, G. S. (2018). Designing Customer-Centric Organisation Structures: Toward the Fluid Marketing Organisation.

13 Shah, Denish, Roland T. Rust, A. Parasuraman, Richard Staelin, and George S. Day (2006), "The Path to Customer Centricity,"

14 Porter, Michael and James Heppelmann (2015), "How Smart, Connected Products Are Transforming Companies,

15 Logan, D., King, J., & Fisher-Wright, H. (2008). Tribal Leadership. Leadership Excellence

16 Levi, D. (2016). Group dynamics for teams

17 Bassot, B. (2016). The reflective practice guide: an interdisciplinary

approach to critical reflection. London: Routledge.

18 Bommaraju, R., Ahearne, M., Krause, R., & Tirunillai, S. (2019). Does a Customer on the Board of Directors Affect Business-to-Business Firm Performance?

19 Cooper, R. G. 1990. Stage-gate systems: A new tool for managing new products

20 Evanschitzky, H. Eisend, M. Calantone, R. Jiang, Y 2012, Success Factors of Product Innovation: An Updated Meta-Analysis

21 Saldanha, T. J. V., Mithas, S., & Krishnan, M. S. (2017). Leveraging Customer Involvement for Fueling Innovation: The Role of Relational and Analytical Information Processing Capabilities

22 Li, Y., Zhang, Y., Xu, J. and Feng, T. (2019), "The impacts of customer involvement on the relationship between relationship quality and performance"

23 Priluck, R. (2003), "Relationship Marketing can mitigate product and service failures", Journal of Services Marketing, Vol. 17 No. 1, pp. 37-52.

24 Lagrosen, S. 2005, Customer Involvement in New Product Development: A Relationship Marketing Perspective.

25 Lagrosen Stefan. (2005). Customer involvement in new product development

26 Curtis, T., Abratt, R., Rhoades, D., & Dion, P. (2011). Customer Loyalty, Repurchase and Satisfaction: A Meta-Analytical Review

27 James, K. W., James, H., Babin, B. J., & Parker, J. M. (2019). Is Customer Satisfaction Really a Catch-All? The Discrepancy between Financial Performance and Survey Results.

28 Henard, D. H., and D. M. Szymanski. 2001. Why some new products are more successful than others

29 Trout, J. (2006, July 3). Peter Drucker On Marketing

30 Chen. (2002). The role of different levels of leadership in predicting self- and collective efficacy: Evidence for discontinuity

31 Woodman, T., Roberts, R., Hardy, L., Callow, N., Rogers, C. H. (2011). There is an "I" in Team: Narcissism and Social Loafing // Research Quarterly for Exercise and Sport. Vol. 82, No. 2, pp. 285–290.

32 Lee, J.-Y., Sridhar, S., Henderson, C. M., & Palmatier, R. W. (2015). Effect of Customer-Centric Structure on Long-Term Financial Performance. Marketing

33 Macleod, L. (2011). Avoiding "group think": A manager's challenge.

Nursing Management. 42(10), 44-48.

34 Jones, G. W., Høigaard, R., Peters, D. M. (2014). "Just Going Through the Motions..": A Qualitative Exploration of Athlete Perceptions of Social Loafing in Training and Competition Contexts – Implications for Team Sport Coaches

35 VVEINHARDT, J., & BANIKONYTĖ, J. (2017). Managerial Solutions that Increase the Effect of Group Synergy and Reduce Social Loafing. Management Of Organisations

36 Deci, E. L., & Ryan, R. M. (2002). Handbook of self-determination research. Rochester, NY: University of Rochester Press.

37 Christie, A., Barling, J., & Turner, N. (2011). Pseudo-transformational leadership: Model specification and outcomes. Journal of Applied Social Psychology, 41(12), 2943–2984.

38 Belbin, R. (2010). Management teams : why they succeed or fail. Amsterdam ; Oxford : Butterworth-Heinemann.

39 Inayat, I. S. (2015). A systematic literature review on agile requirements engineering practices and challenges.

40 Bjarnason, E., Wnuk, K., & Regnell, B. (2011a). A case study on benefits and side effects of agile practices in large-scale requirements engineering. in Agile RE.

41 O'DOHERTY, D., & Vachhani, S. (2017). Individual differences, personalities and self. In D. Knights, Introducing Organisational Behaviour and Management

42 Cohen , B., & Thias, M. (2009). The Failure of the Off-shore Experiment: A Case for Collocated Agile Teams. Agile Conference, AGILE '09, 251.

43 Stephen, D. (2015). Updating the Agile Manifesto. Strategy & Leadership

44 Hertzberg, F. (2003). One more time: How do you motivate employees? Harvard Business Review on Motivating people, Boston, MA: Harvard Business School Press

45 Gardner, H. K. (2012). Performance pressure as a double-edged sword: Enhancing team motivation but undermining the use of team knowledge. Administrative Science Quarterly, 57(1), 1-46.

46 Eberlain , A., & Julio Cesar, S. (2002). Agile requirements definition: A view from requirements engineering. In Proceedings of the international workshop on time constrained requirements engineerin

47 Angus-Leppan, T., Metcalf, L., & Benn, S. (2010). Leadership Styles

and CSR Practice

48   Bass, B. M., & Riggio, R. E. (2006). Transformational leadership

49   Manz, C. C., & Sims, H. P. (1991). Superleadership beyond the myth of Heroic leadership. Orgnizational Dynamics, 19(4): 18-35.

50   Barling, J., Christie, A., & Turner, N. (2008). Pseudo-transformational leadership: Towards the development and test of a model. Journal of Business Ethics, 81(4), 851–861.

51   Kark, R., Shamir, B., & Chen, G. (2013). The two faces of transformational leadership: Empowerment and dependency

52   Angus-Leppan, T., Metcalf, L., & Benn, S. (2010). Leadership Styles and CSR Practice: An Examination of Sensemaking

53   Lin, C. S., Huang, P. C., Chen, S. J., & Huang, S. C. (2017). Pseudo-transformational Leadership is in the Eyes of the Subordinates. Journal Of Business Ethics, 141(1), 179-190. doi:10.1007/s10551-015-2739-5.

54   Barling, J., Christie, A., & Turner, N. (2008). Pseudo-transformational leadership: Towards the development and test of a model

55   Highsmith, J., & Fowler, M. (2001). The Agile Manifesto. Software Development, 9(8), 29-30.

56   Gagne, M., & Deci, E. (2005). Self-determination theory and work motivation. Journal of Organisational Behavior, 26, 331–362.

57   Chen. (2002). The role of different levels of leadership in predicting self- and collective efficacy: Evidence for discontinuity

58   Zoethout, K., Jager, W., & Molleman, E. (2007). Task dynamics in self-organising task groups: expertise, motivational, and performance differences of Chen, F., Zhang, L., Latimer, J. (2014).

59   Hayes, N. (1997). Successful team management. London, UK: International Thomson Business Press.

60   Van Vugt, M., Jepson, S., Hart, C., & De Cremer, D. (2004). Autocratic Leadership in Social Dilemmas

61   Edmondson, A., & Nembhard, I. (2009). Product development and learning in project teams: The challenges are the benefits. Journal of Product Innovation Management, 26, 123-138.

62   Pink, D. H. (2010). Drive: The surprising truth about what motivates us

63   Perry, S. J., Lorinkova, N. M., Hunter, E. M., Hubbard, A., McMahon, J. T. (2016). When does Virtuality Really "Work"? Examining the Role of Work–Family and Virtuality in Social Loafing

64 Stark, E. M., Shaw, J. D., Duffy, M. K. (2007). Preference for Group Work, Winning Orientation, and Social Loafing Behavior in Groups // Group & Organisation Management. Vol. 32, No. 6, pp. 699–723.

65 Goold, M., & Campbell, A. (2002, March 1). Do you have a well-designed organisation? Harvard Business Review. https://hbr.org/2002/03/do-you-have-a-well-designed-organisation

66 Ferrante, C. J., Green, S. G., Forster, W. R. (2006). Getting More Out of Team Projects: Incentivizing Leadership to Enhance Performance // Journal of Management Education. Vol. 30, No. 6, pp. 788–797.

67 Dibrell, Clay, Justin B. Craig, and Donald O. Neubaum. 2014. Linking the Formal Strategic Planning Process, Planning Flexibility, and Innovativeness to Firm Performance

68 Mintzberg, Henry. 1994. The Fall and Rise of Strategic Planning

69 Porter, Michael E and James E Heppelmann (2015), "How Smart, Connected Products Are Transforming Companies," (accessed February 15, 2020)

70 McFarlane, Donovan A. (2013) "The Strategic Importance of Customer Value,"

71 Liozu, S. M. (2017). Customer Value Is Not Just Created, It Is Formally Managed

72 Keller, K. L. 1993. "Conceptualizing, Measuring and Managing Customer-Based Brand Equity." Journal of Marketing 57:1–22.–89.

73 Anderson, E. T., & Kumar, N. (2007). Price competition with repeat, loyal buyers

74 T. Yao, X. Fan, Q. Zheng and L. Mu, "A Meta-Analysis of Value-Driven Service Customer Satisfaction," 2010

75 James, K. W., James, H., Babin, B. J., & Parker, J. M. (2019). Is Customer Satisfaction Really a Catch-All? The Discrepancy between Financial Performance and Survey Results

76 Golovkova, A. (1), Malova, A. (1), Podkorytova, O. (1,3), & Eklof, J. (2). (n.d.). Customer satisfaction index and financial performance: a European cross country study

77 Rust, R. T., T. Ambler, G. S. Carpenter, V. A. Kumar, and R. J. Srivastava. 2004. "Measuring Marketing Productivity: Current Knowledge and Future Directions." Journal of Marketing

78 Verbeeten, F. H. M., & Vijn, P. (2010). Are Brand-Equity Measures Associated with Business-Unit Financial Performance? Empirical Evidence from the Netherlands. Journal of Accounting, Auditing &